About the Book

The book of "Opinions" was written to pass on to others the thoughts of one individual who loves the United States and would like for his grandchildren to experience freedoms at least equal to the freedoms he had while living in this great country. Some of the opinions also offer possible solutions to problems and issues that continue to plague our society and our government. The author has used his education, 62 plus years of life experiences, and fairness in writing his opinions. If you are interested in freedom and equality this book offers the reader a look at what was, what is, and what could be.

I0416508

For Love Of Country
"OPINIONS"

by

Ray Reeves

authorHOUSE

1663 Liberty Drive, Suite 200
Bloomington, Indiana 47403
(800) 839-8640
www.authorhouse.com

First published by AuthorHouse 09/01/04

ISBN: 1-4184-7708-7 (sc)

Printed in the United States of America
Bloomington, Indiana

This book is printed on acid-free paper.

Table of Contents

Chapter One The Lucky Generation 1

Chapter Two Government and Politics 24

Chapter Three Taxes 36

Chapter Four New World Order 49

Chapter Five Race Relations................... 61

Chapter Six Religion 80

Chapter Seven Potpourri 100

FOREWORD

This foreword is dedicated to the people who want to write about their beliefs, feelings, and thoughts but think no one will care what they think. That, in its self, matters very little. What matters is that your ideas have been applied to the written page and you have not kept them bottled up inside where only you will know of them. Others who may someday read them will know some of your thoughts and ideas. Think of the millions of thoughts and ideas lost forever over time because people like you and me never bothered to write them down.

Being published in today's world is not as important as it once was as the computer age allows everyone the opportunity to be his or her own publisher. I realize this book will probably never be published by a commercial publisher but I can publish it myself one copy at a time if necessary. You can do the same with your book. There are publishers out there that will publish books at a cost to the writer.

I would like to be able to say that many who read this will not agree with much of what I write. I cannot, however, say many, as probably very few will read even one chapter let alone the whole book. All of us, as normal human beings (some may think of me as abnormal), have the ability to think and reason. Very few of us think or reason the same way by using the same information each of us gather in our daily lives. This is what makes us unique as individuals.

What I ask of those who do read this book is to keep an open mind and not shut me off because of something I wrote that you might not agree with. I promise I will do the same if I read your book someday. If there are areas where you can agree with me or perhaps say that I have a point of view similar to the way you think then we have an understanding. If what I write makes you think or even changes your mind then I consider this a worthwhile effort. If what I write offends you then I apologize for the offense but not for the writing of my opinion.

I have selected several areas (chapters) of issues and ideas that I feel strongly about or that have plagued our society for too long. Some are areas that I do not believe will be widely accepted or appreciated. For those of you who can relate to what I write you will know you are not alone in your thoughts and ideas.

When thinking about a title my first thought was, "Who is Ray Reeves, and why the hell do I care what he thinks". As you can see that is a really long title so I decided on a shorter title simply called, "Opinions". We all have them and these are mine.

My writing comes mostly from remembering what I have read, watched on TV, or learned through my 60 plus years. I am basically lazy and will not do a lot of factual research and bore the reader with pages and pages of references and quotes. I could not, and would not, try to write without the help of the computer. The computer is both saint and devil to our society but it is of our time.

You will notice that I frequently reference the government in most of the chapters. I have strong feelings about our present government as compared to what I believe the Founding Fathers had in mind for government. I believe they have become far too intrusive in our daily lives and continue to pass laws that are very questionable as to their constitutionality.

I am not a writer by any stretch of the imagination. I do not have a real command of the English language even though it is my native language. I have no one to blame for this except myself for not properly learning while in school. So even though I have the computer's help you may still find grammatical errors. I am hopeful that the computer and I have caught any spelling errors. However, if you can understand what I am saying then that will be good enough for me.

This will be in my own words and style. I think that is what Charles Schulz done with his wonderful cartoons. In one of his cartoons, I think it was Charlie Brown who was having trouble learning punctuation and like me could not grasp all the rules so he lined up a bunch of punctuation symbols and ask us to use them where we wanted them. So with that in mind, !!!,,,....?????""'':::::;;;;;"""""", enjoy.

Ray Reeves, Austin, Texas

Chapter One
<u>The Lucky Generation</u>

I have started with this chapter so you can have a better idea of when I started. It may allow more insight as to how I came to have my views that are expressed in this and later chapters. I have also typed it in an 18-point font so many of us from the lucky generation can perhaps read it without our bifocals. In addition, the larger print will allow me to have more pages and a larger book. I know some folks are impressed with size. If published commercially it may not be in an 18-point font.

The first thing needed is for me to qualify a generation. To me a generation is any period of time from birth to the average time of those born creating the next generation by having their own children. This can cover a number of years so there is no exact amount of time that constitutes a generation. The life experience of each generation may extend into several more generations but a generation all have the most in common with each other.

Those of us born after the Great Depression through the end of the Korean War are probably the luckiest generation ever born in the United States of America. This of course would not include the ones who lost loved ones in WWII and Korea until the hurt of the loss faded and they resumed their lives. A few from the lucky generation may have given their lives in Korea. Unfortunately, these heroes never really had an opportunity to enjoy their lives in the lucky generation. However, they did what they believed to be right to try and stop the spread of communism. To all the brave souls who fought and died or came back maimed from the wars I am thankful for their great sacrifice.

Since I did not live in the generations before this period of time I can only make my observations based on the history I have read, seen on TV, or been told about by those who did experience the prior generations. Since I have lived in the generations during and after my generation I have my own experience and education with which to base my observations and opinions. There were probably a lot of good periods of time before the lucky generation, however, I think the bad times then, compared to the later times, far out weigh the good times.

The first settlers were not actually born in this country, and some came as a commercial venture but they were the ones who set down the foundation. I don't think I would have liked to live in this country in the 17th century. I think those times must have really been hard. I am not the type that would have found it enjoyable to work from daylight to dark trying to scratch out a living and make a home for the family. Surviving the cold winters, fighting with the Native Americans, and making almost everything by hand is not my idea of fun. I believe those who came to this country as the founders thought it was better than what they left in Europe or they probably would not have made the journey. I wonder how many thought they had made a mistake by the end of the first year. However, I am very thankful for the sacrifices they made as it allowed our great country to become a reality.

As others came and the first born in this country lived their generations I know they must have also experienced many hard times. I have to believe more bad than good. I would not liked to have lived here before a more modern time. Travel by walking, by horse, or by wagon is far too slow. Farming by following a couple of mules or oxen in a field is not my idea of a way to enjoy life. Even the wealthy of those times did not live as good as most of the poor of the lucky generation. Living under a King's rule is not appealing to me either. We no longer have the King, but the tax issue is still with us. As the country continued to grow so did, in most cases, an easier life evolve.

Historically, the time of the revolutionary era may have been a great time to have lived. One would have had an opportunity to help the Republic form and win independence from England. One may have been able to rub elbows with many of the great men who put all their worldly possessions on the line to let the following generations live in such a great nation. One may have been a framer of the constitution and signed the Declaration of Independence. That would have been such a great honor. Be thankful for and always honor those who provided us with the freedoms and opportunities we citizens now have in this great country. After the Revolutionary War the country now had a new vision but a lot of work was yet to be accomplished.

The period that brought forth the countries greatest president had a lot more to offer than earlier periods as far as technical advances and the Republic had several decades of being a nation under its belt. Even with this I would not liked to have lived to watch the nation become divided and see fathers, brothers, and sometimes whole families killed in a war so terrible that the whole of the population suffered in some manner.

Personally, I think the war was justified even with all of the carnage, as no people should have to live under the banner of slavery. No one has the right to own another as a slave; especially in a country that had freedom written so deeply in its roots.

I am so thankful for the strong will and determination of President Lincoln to make right the wrong of slavery. It took a strong man to suffer the trials and tribulations this man went through. He was either loved or hated for his stand on slavery. I am also thankful that he felt so strongly about reuniting the nation after the war. I regret such a great leader never lived to see some of what his hard worked brought forth.

Reconstruction did not bring forth the life that was promised to the freed slaves and that probably would not have happened if President Lincoln's life had not been cut short by a group of conspirators. The president that followed could have made sure the promises were kept but instead, due to his own view on slavery and the political pressure, he allowed the injustice to the freedmen to continue. Thankfully, he later got his comeuppance.

The hatred and turmoil that followed the Civil War in my opinion would not have been a good time to have lived. More than 600,000 Americans lost their lives in the war. The most of any war that the Republic has ever been involved in to include WWII. Few families escaped with out losing a friend or loved one. Many had lost their homes during the war so a lot of survivors headed west to try and build a new life.

Was the war worth the pain and suffering? I will leave you to answer that in your own way but I believe freeing the slaves and reuniting the Republic was the right thing to do.

Shortly, in terms of history, this country was in the biggest industrial and land expansion ever seen in the history of the world. Much of this expansion can be attributed to the Civil War. Lots of good things were happening except for the Western Native Americans. They were being steadily driven off lands where they had lived for centuries. Even though they had battled other tribes over lands it was a hard concept to understand land ownership the way the white man understood land ownership. Of course, the white man prevailed and I don't think the Native Americans got a fair shake in the east or out west.

If I had lived in another generation I think the generation between the 1870s and the 1890s would have been the one I would choose. Things were still tough and life was still hard compared to our more modern times but the sense of adventure and opportunities open to Americans would have made it an exciting time to have lived from my point of view. The west was wide open and anyone with the courage could build a great future. Even with this I still think it would not have been as good as the lucky generation.

A lot of great things were happening in the Republic at the turn of the century. More modern homes and more conveniences. More merchandise of all types to buy instead of spending hours and days to make. Cities allowed the option of many different careers. People rapidly changed from being farmers and living off the land to working for others for a wage. Trains were entering their prime and people could travel in hours and days to places that had taken days, weeks, and months just a few years earlier. Electricity was beginning to light homes and businesses. There were more opportunities for education. Automobiles began replacing the horse and buggy. Farmers would soon be tilling the land with tractors while the mules watched from retirement. Machinery was allowing manufacturing to turn out an endless supply of items that made life easier. Things were better for sure.

However, things were still not good for all, as women were still not legally allowed to vote and most African Americans did not vote due to intimidation, poll taxes, and any other means that white men could come up with. So the white man was in the catbird seat making all the rules. For some there was still a lot left to be desired.

The early to late twenties may have been an exciting time to have lived. WWI had ended and the country was back to growing and enjoying life. The nation had gotten through women's suffrage and they could now vote and hold office. This brought more viewpoints to the table for shaping the Republic even though most women still maintained a low profile when it came to politics. Men had to accept the fact that they and they alone, no longer were the only voice.

Entertainment and the time to enjoy it were everywhere. People who lived in larger cities could go to moving pictures, dances, plays, and even wild nightclubs. People out west had barn dances, barbeques, rodeos, occasional traveling shows, and some towns even had opera houses. People had a lot more options for enjoying life.

Then came the Great Depression. The Republic had experienced depressions before and since but nothing compared to the big one. It was felt worldwide. The depression era would have been a miserable time to have lived. The strong and determined survived the depression and they are to be highly admired in my book. I am not sure the present generations could endure the hardships lived by those generations. I hope none of them will ever have to face anything even close.

My Mother and Dad lived through this period. They both told their children stories that we believed. They were not the stories from the history books. These were real stories about family, friends, and neighbors and the hard times they shared. One thing the depression did was to bring most people closer together. Many shared meager means with complete strangers as everyone was in the same boat.

That is one of the great attributes of the American people. They seem to cast aside all differences and unite during catastrophes or hard times when others are in need. 9-11-01 was a tragic time for the Republic but for a time you could see the great unity and love for our country. It is sad that we don't live like this without the tragedies.

During the depression even the wealthy suffered to some extent, as many things they were use to having were no longer available as they were no longer being made. Fifty cents to a dollar a day from sun to sun was a common wage if you could even find a job. The survivors, our grandparents and parents, lived through a terrible part of their lives but they came out strong and determined to continue building the Republic and the New Deal was the main catalyst. We owe those generations a great deal of admiration and respect. Just think of all the great accomplishment in the New Deal era. There were so many, but if you have ever stood on top of the Hoover Dam then you will know of what I write. Even with the help of the New Deal that pulled the Republic out of the depression it was not a time that I would liked to have experienced.

That brings us to why I think my generation was the lucky generation. Here I want to qualify what I mean in terms of lucky. By lucky I mean that the improvement in the quality of life and freedom to enjoy it without today's fears and problems or the harder times of the past.

I was born just prior to WWII but the war did not affect me in any way that I can remember. Many born during this generation were affected by the war. They lost fathers, brothers, and other family members. Some were separated from their loved ones for long lengths of time.

My Dad did not have to go to the war even though he tried to volunteer. I guess this was lucky for him and the family. When he went to the draft board to volunteer he was in his late twenties. He had three children with a fourth on the way. This, in and of itself, would not have prevented him from going but when the draft board considered this along with his civilian occupation they told him that he was more valuable on the home front.

Dad was a tire recapper and there were no new tires available to the general public during much of the war. The only tires civilians and regular businesses could get were recaps. All the new tires supported the war effort. This was the case with many commodities. My Dad was a very patriotic citizen and I often wondered how not being able to fight for his country affected him in life. I know he was very proud of four sons and a daughter who later served in the military.

After the war, look out, man did things ever start happening. The soldiers returned with opportunities to start families or reunite with family. Schooling was available for any of them who wanted to pursue it. Jobs soon become plentiful due to all of the manufacturing and construction. Suburbs sprang up everywhere and the GI Bill allowed millions the opportunity to own homes for a reasonable price. Food and other consumer products were soon rolling off the assembly lines and the ration stamps became a thing of the past. Times were truly good and getting better each passing day.

After the death of President Roosevelt who gets the credit for getting the Republic out of the depression we got another pretty good president that accepted the responsibilities of the office and proclaimed to the world that "The Buck Stops Here". Unfortunately, much of President

Truman's time was consumed by the later war in Korea. Some even wanted him impeached for the way he conducted the war.

By the end of the 40s the efforts of the nation was aimed toward making life easier with more time to enjoy the new conveniences coming to the market place. Many of the women that had work so hard and long in the factories during the war were now getting married, having babies, and staying home to raise them. Most children in those days came home from school to find Mom there and ready to fix them a snack and help with their homework. Mom didn't even have to go pick them up, as it was safe for them to walk or ride their bicycle home without fear of being abducted or shot in a drive-by. It was a time when the teachers were still allowed to control the classroom and the "Pledge of Allegiance" was recited daily. Prayer was even allowed in schools but was not needed then near as much as it is now. It was BFI (before federal intervention).

Automobiles started coming out with automatic transmissions and soon some would even have air conditioning. New homes were almost all built with inside plumbing and the four rooms and a path were rapidly turning into six rooms and a bath. Some of us will remember the path and the two holer at the end, with the Sears Roebuck catalog and the fear of the black widow spiders or snakes down below. Soon most homes, even in the rural areas, had inside plumbing and most did not have to wait long for electricity. The old kerosene lamps were put in storage and the stink left the house.

Into the 50s the modernization continued. Homes all over the country, not just in the big cities, began seeing the living room with a television and the family gathered around in the evenings watching this modern miracle. The shows then were decent and entertaining and parents could allow the children to watch without fear of them seeing a nude scene or having to listen to the F-word. I find nothing wrong with shows like "Leave it to Beaver" or "Father knows best". They were wholesome, funny, and very typical of the way many families lived as a family unit. Ward and June Cleaver were always there for Wally and the Beaver. Even when the mischievous Eddy Haskell would talk the Beaver into a mischievous act the parents were there to get him out of trouble or put him on the right path.

Did that show influence the actors? I think so as they all turned out pretty good even after the acting careers ended. The real Eddy Haskell even dedicated his life as a civil servant in the Los Angeles area as a police officer or so it has been told. During this period I cannot help but believe the evenings spent with the family in front of the TV brought the families closer together.

On Saturday afternoons children could go to the matinee for a couple of milk bottle caps as admission and if you didn't have the bottle caps the admission was only a dime. In most theaters a nice size bag of popcorn was only a nickel. The matinees were usually a double feature with a weekly serial and a couple of cartoons. This gave Mom time to do some shopping, as many Dads had to work until at least noon on Saturday. Then later when the movie was over the parents would pick up the children from the movie in the old Ford or Chevy. In the small towns it was just fine if the children walked home to a house where the front door was unlocked. There was little worry that some petty thief would rip you off to get money for their next fix.

The early 50s brought us into another war even though officially it was referred to as a conflict. Somewhat like the later Vietnam war, diplomatically, we were involved in the late 40s. The Korean War was not the worst time for the lucky generation but would have to be considered a really bad time especially for those who had to fight there. Most of my generation did not actually get involved in the fighting in Korea but a few may have toward the end of the war. However, some of this generation did lose family members. There was close to 54,000 Americans who lost their lives in Korea. Many have referred to Korea as "The Forgotten War".

The war lasted about three years and even though it was not as long as some wars we have been involved in it was a terribly hard war to fight. This was due to the bitter cold winters, the terrain, and the fact that after the Chinese got involved our military was forced to retreat with high casualties. This was something the U.S. Military had rarely ever faced and it caused morale problems. We later retook a lot of what was lost in the retreat and the Koreas were divided at the 38th parallel where tensions still exist more than a half a century later. This was the first major war since the founding of the United Nations and there were many UN troops who also fought and died in Korea.

Even with high casualties it could have been worse. Due to advances in medical technology and an improved evacuation system many of the wounded survived the war that probably would not have survived in previous wars. I think the Mobil Army Surgical Hospitals (MASH) were the main reason for the survival rate. I don't think the doctors, nurses, and support personnel ever received the official recognition they deserved but the later acclaimed TV series M*A*S*H gave them well deserved recognition. Even though it was a Hollywood version and meant to be humorous it still recognized the job they did to save American and allied lives during the war. I don't know how realistic the Hollywood version was but some that were there have said it wasn't too far off. I know the episodes where the bitter cold of the winters made life miserable was true because I experienced some of that bitter cold on a Navy ship off the coast of Korea in the 60s.

I guess the ex-general elected to the presidency in 1952 will have to get the credit for ending our involvement in the war. About all he did the rest of the 50s was to play golf and let us enjoy the good times. He did have some involvement in the very early activities leading up to the Vietnam War. Ho Chi Minh was trying to liberate French Indonesia (Vietnam) from the French. He was unsuccessful at gaining any support from the West so he turned to the communist for help. This automatically made him an enemy of the West. Of course the USSR and China were only too happy to give him help. I have wondered what may have happened if we would have been more aggressive in a political manner in the early stages. Of course when the French pulled out in the middle 50s after fighting Ho for several years he was considered a communist by all of the free world. This almost assured that our involvement would be greater in the days to come.

The middle 50s brought our generation some of the greatest automobiles and music that had ever been seen or heard. It was every teenager's dream to own a 55, 56, or 57 Chevy. The 55 and 56 Ford Crown Vic were also a very desirable model. We were the first to see and be able to drive the Corvette and Thunderbird. Of course few of us could afford one as teenagers but many drove them later and they remain classics even today. A well equipped 57 Chevy two door Hardtop in 1957 would have been obtainable for about $3000.00. Today the same Chevy in pristine condition can fetch as much as $40 to $50 thousand as an example of how great they are. The lucky generation started Rock and Roll and there was no better music or performers before or since than the music that came out of the 50s and 60s. They were so many greats that it makes me dizzy to even try and mention them but some of my favorites were The Platters, The Supremes, The King, Fats Domino, Chubby Checker, Little Richard, Buddy Holly, The Big Bopper and on and on and on. Even though I listened to a lot of CW music also in those days that early Rock and Roll was the greatest. I was no longer a teen by the time the Beatles hit our shores but they continued our music. If you do not believe what I tell you about our music just ask anyone from that generation and they will verify the truth.

When JFK received enough votes and defeated Nixon for the presidency in 1960 many of us thought we had finally hit pay dirt with a great leader. JFK came into the office with high hopes and big dreams for the Republic. He did become a very popular president. Shortly after coming into office he was faced with the Cuban crisis. He made some enemies among the high ranking military members, as they wanted him to start bombing right away. Even though he made enemies among some of the senior officers I think most of the lower ranking officers and the enlisted men really admired him.

After JFK became president we got to see Americans go into space, faster and faster computers, everyone getting color TVs, nice cars, homes with washing machines, dish washers, telephones in every room, at least two baths in most homes and so many more new affordable conveniences. We were given opportunities to get rich that had never before been possible. Computers had become a definite reality that has led to an information giant. The modern airline industry made travel to anywhere in the world affordable and very fast. One didn't have to go through six layers of security to board the plane and you could even greet a friend named Jack. The military could fly standby for half price. That was a perk I took advantage of but really never thanked the airline industry so I will thank them now.

Then came Vietnam. Very few decades have passed when the Republic was not involved in some kind of war. This probably says something about us as a nation. I guess you can consider this as my generation's war. For sure it was the worse thing that happened to the lucky generation. Many of us from the lucky generation served in this war. Many lost their lives and many families lost their loved ones. Most of us believed what we were doing there was right. However, after we failed to win due to politics many of us had second thoughts. Not about trying to keep the South free but the way the politicians allowed the war to be fought.

Actually, the U.S. was involved fairly deep in a diplomatic way before President Kennedy came into office so he inherited the Vietnam situation. This Vietnam issue plagued JFK he whole time he was president. I think he was truly trying to find a way to get us out of Vietnam when he was assassinated. Some theorist thinks his desire to get out of Vietnam was one of the reasons he was assassinated. Of course there is no factual proof of that. We will probably never know the real truth as to a conspiracy or just a cowardly little nut wanting to make a place in history. I want to believe the latter is probably the most likely.

I believe his loss to the Republic did something to the hopes and dreams of the American people. I guess we suffered the same kind of loss that so many suffered when President Lincoln was assassinated. I don't think the Republic has been the same since that tragic day in November, 1963.

I have often wondered where we would be as a nation today if JFK had been able to serve two terms. Yes, I know about some of his indiscretions and the rumors of being tied to organized crime. I believe the part about the sex but I do not believe the organized crime part as Bobby was close to Jack and Bobby waged war on organized crime as Attorney General. If Clinton's indiscretions and lies can be overlooked then we can surly overlook JFK's also. At least JFK was never impeached. I think he was our second best president considering the amount of time he served.

It seems that since then hook and crook has led us. A citizen can no longer believe anything the government tells us. Oh, I know you people who thought Reagan was so great will question and disagree with that, but it is my opinion. I will give President Reagan the biggest of ovations for thawing the cold war and I think this is his finest legacy. In 1960 serving in Germany I never expected to see a free East Germany in my lifetime.

It sure didn't take long after LBJ took over that the war really escalated. A lot of people may disagree with me but the politicians in office who supported and helped LBJ after the Gulf of Tonkin Resolution have the blood of all the Americans killed and wounded on their hands. I hold him, his cabinet, and the members of congress who helped him completely responsible for the defeat in the war and the division of the Republic.

It was not the ability of our armed forces that led to the defeat it was the restrictions placed on them by the politicians that led to the defeat. The real enemy was the lack of resolve and proper action by the politicians. LBJ was given a full mandate to stop the aggression by congress in the Gulf of Tonkin Resolution. Of course now, many believe the incidents that formed the bases for the resolution never happened. His decisions that tied the hands of the military and his lack of resolve to bomb the enemy into submission caused the defeat.

The defeat was not a military defeat it was strictly a political defeat that caused over 50,000 Americans to lose their lives. I also think he had other options besides war but there was a lot of money to be made with a war. Just ask some of the contractors who built the bases in Vietnam.

To the ones who lost their lives and to their loved ones, to the sons and daughters who never knew their fathers, to the veterans who came back wounded both physically and spiritually, I am so truly sorry that such poor leaders caused you so much pain and sorrow.

The generations that fought the Vietnam War, many of us from the lucky generation, ended up in a very different USA. So even with the wars, when I think back to all the good times growing up in the 40s, 50s, and early 60s that the prior generations never had. When I remember the serenity, safety, and the love of the Republic that must have been some of what inspired Norman Rockwell's paintings of small town America. When I look forward at the now generation with all of the "ME" attitude and to future generations with the problems they face. When I see the deceit in government, corporations, businesses, and individuals. When I see the desire by so many, especially within our government and educational institutions for a New World order with a one-world government that will completely destroy the sovereignty of the Republic. When I see the freedom we have lost with the "Patriot Act" (a complete theft of our Bill of Rights). Then I can conclude that in my opinion my generation was the Lucky Generation.

I feel sorry for my grandchildren; Lindsey, Lauren, Tayler, Marissa, Garrett, and Justin, who may never experience a full lifetime in the United States of America that the founding fathers envisioned or even that I was lucky enough to have experienced. I feel sorry for them knowing that the United Nations may someday control their lives. A body of world leaders where half are dictators of third world nations that know nothing or care nothing of a citizen's freedoms. I have been wrong many times about many things and I truly hope that I am wrong about the UN, however, evidence points that we are headed in that direction.

I may be in violation of the patriot act by writing this opinion and I may even be labeled as a terrorist by the government. But like many before me I will take that chance in order to express my opinion in accordance with my rights under the first amendment of the constitution of the United States of America.

Though most of us have not seen or experienced any drastic changes in our daily freedoms associated with the patriot act, it is a tool the government can use to take all our freedoms away virtually overnight. So I caution all of you to keep a close eye on the government, as they are suppose to bow unto the citizens, not the other way around.

Chapter Two
<u>Government and Politics</u>

Government is too big and Politics too rotten. And from there it gets worse.

When the Republic was founded the founding fathers had a great vision of government. If we could return to just double what was originally planned we would be just fine.

Instead, the government has grown so large and is so bureaucratic that no one knows what is going on in the office next door. The catalyst that propels the growth and bureaucracy is **Power**. Each department wants its own empire.

Since the beginning of time man has desired power. I know of no exceptions except one who is mentality challenged and even then, depending on the severity, the mentality challenged has even sought power. The cave man wanted power and control over his mate. He even wanted and needed power over the prey he sought for food. If you are so inclined you can even go back beyond the caveman to the primates and there you will find the leaders who exerted power over the rest of the troop.

This desire and need for power has not changed and it overpowers all else for those who seek to become more powerful. That is why we have a government today that is completely out of control when it comes to doing what is in the best interest of the Republic and the Republic's citizens who is suppose to be the controlling force over government. The citizen's lack of controlling the government is what has allowed the government to get so large and powerful that the government now controls the citizens.

The government was set up to have three branches. The Legislative (Congress), the Executive (President and Cabinet) and the Judicial (Supreme Court). Simply put, the legislative job was to represent the people and to make laws to protect commerce, safety, and civil obedience of the people as they were spread far and wide and could not feasibly represent themselves. The job of the executive was to approve the laws passed by the legislative branch, represent the United States in foreign affairs and be the Commander in Chief of the military. The job of the judicial was to make sure the laws passed by the legislative branch and approved by the executive branch were constitutional.

Where did it all go wrong? That is the question. Trying to figure out this problem is so easy that it is almost impossible to accomplish. It went wrong when the people allowed the branches of the government to become too powerful. We the people did not fire the representatives when they failed to represent our best interest. We allowed them to do what they thought would be best for us but usually included them gaining power. They made laws that protected them and gave them the ability to increase their office staffs, cabinet members, and power. We laid back and took it like chumps. After a while when they seen how easy it was to run over us they continued to do so. They have been doing it so long now that they have become real experts. They have in place now every scheme in the book, and some not yet tried, to keep the power for themselves and continue to abuse the people with higher taxes, unnecessary laws that restrict our rights, and rewards them with outlandish retirement benefits while we struggle to make ends meet.

How many senators or representatives have ever been voted out of office? Not very many I assure you. What is even worse is that most were elected into office by less than twenty-five percent of the eligible voters in their districts. If one did happen to get voted out of office they just turned around and became a lobbyist. They do so many favors for the special interest that contributes to their campaigns that they have no time to work for the people and we set back and allow it to happen.

Some of us that are a little more aware set around and talk about what they are doing but very few of us ever try to boot them out of office by voting. Too many of us say that we don't vote because our vote doesn't count. Well that is only true when it comes to the president. The Electoral College can put a president in office that was not numerically elected by the people but this rarely if ever happens. All other elected officials can be controlled very effectively by the vote, but only if the people vote.

When we stay complacent about the job they do for us they will not work except in their best interest. Do you know of any federal level elected official that has not retired a rich person? Granted, a lot of them have gotten into office because they have money but they leave with a whole lot more. I could name you a couple from Texas.

Perhaps, politics in smaller communities for school boards, mayor, council people, and such are good honest folks with the best interest of the community in mind. Part of the evidence for this is that in many small towns most of the jobs are not paid positions. Also, most of these people are just plain folks. You may have the local barber, grocery clerk or office worker in these offices. The farther up the political ladder the dirtier and more ruthless politics become because the higher it goes the more powerful the office becomes. The higher it goes the better chance that there is going to be a professional politician in that office and many times it is lawyers. When you cross lawyers and politicians into one then you have problems ahead. Look at our modern day congress for evidence.

In a small town each individual has direct access to the politicians. If the mayor won't see you in his office then you can catch him at the grocery store or the service station or any number of places and let him or her know what is on your mind. The larger the town, the more difficult it is to have access. The politicians are masters at putting so many layers of protection such as secretaries and aids in place that it is almost impossible to reach them. With the modern telephone systems you will be lucky if you can even talk to a real human when you try to reach the powers to be.

About the only way you have of controlling your access to the politicians is through the ballot box. The problem here is that too few citizens care enough to take an hour out of their day to go vote. Most communities now have absentee voting that allows people to vote at their own convenience and even that has not increased the vote significantly.

I live in a medium size city and it has approximately 500,000 voters and the total votes in mayoral and city council elections are less than 12% and many times less than 10%. County, State and Federal elections are about the same. People, this is not the way to run the government. The elected officials must know that the voters will turn out and fire them if they do not govern the way most of the community wants them to govern. Almost any politician can run on a particular issue such as the environment and have a certain amount of voters in their corner. So when the elections come about and the voters for a particular candidate with whom they agree runs for the office they turn out in full and get him or her elected because the voters who may not like the politician or what they represent just flat won't go and vote to stop the special interest group. That is how 10% of the community controls the other 90% that are too lazy to vote.

How can the non-voters be encouraged to vote? If I knew the answer to that I wouldn't have time to write this book. I think there are ways in which we can increase voter participation in this modern age of communications. I can see no good reason why we cannot vote through computers or even the telephone to an electronic system. After all, many voting machines today are computerized.

Some say that the computer and telephone can be manipulated and the true results may not be so true. It is no more dangerous than the manual ballot box. You see, in most local elections and it actually goes all the way to the federal elections a County Clerk or Secretary of State runs the elections. These people are from a particular political party. The two largest parties are the Democrats and Republicans. So usually these elected or appointed positions are one or the other. When the ballot boxes are picked up from the polling places they are usually picked up by people selected by the person in charge, i.e., The County Clerk. They are then stored in a place controlled by his or her office and staff. The votes are then counted by people selected by the office in charge. Very few protection devices are in place to prevent the count from being manipulated. In an election in Texas for a particular senate seat years ago it was found later that dead people had voted for the one who won the election. Go figure!

More and more elections are having votes tallied by electronic tallying machines (computers). Even with this the party in charge of the election process is still involved with the tally machines. I would rather trust my vote going from my computer or my telephone directly into a central computer somewhere not controlled by any party. I think that programs can be developed today with the necessary safeguards to prevent manipulation or false voting. This could probably be done by having the social security account number (SSAN) the factor that would let the computer know that you were old enough to vote, that you had not yet voted in the present election, and that you are an eligible voter. A pin number or something similar could be used in conjunction with the SSAN to assure no one could just obtain a list of SSANs and use them to vote for their candidate.

I really think that a more modern voting application would encourage more people to vote. It is also time for us to modernize the voting process as to prevent the fiasco we witnessed in Florida during the 2000 presidential election. Here we are in the 21st century and we still have hanging chads and ballots that can not be read by voters. This is absolutely absurd.

Besides so many of the elected officials at the state and federal level being lawyers another very large problem is the party system we have in the Republic. Too many citizens vote the party line and I cannot for the life of me understand why supposedly intelligent people will be so loyal to a party instead of voting for candidates that are running for the office. I know one has to register for a particular party for purpose of the primary but that does not mean they have to vote just for candidates in that party in the general elections. Personally, I vote for the candidate that I think will do the most towards things that I want. Sometimes that may be a democrat, republican, independent, green, or even a libertarian.

Money is another large problem that I think the citizen's should do something about. The cost today in a presidential election is obscene. I know congress makes the rules on elections but I believe the people can bring about enough pressure on their senators and representatives that we can get election financing reformed to the point where an intelligence average citizen could actually run for the presidential office. At present the parties, their wealth, or ability to raise money and a powerful person within the party are the only ones that stand even a ghost of a chance of running, let alone, getting elected.

One method that could work is to not allow any personal funds to be used. Not allow any corporations to donate to a campaign. Not allow any monies from the parties. Set a limit of $100.00 as the maximum contribution that anyone could make and only individuals could donate. No other organization of any kind would be allowed to contribute. This would insure that any candidate could run and would have to run a campaign where his or her message would be the main factor in getting elected. Yes, there could still be some party influence under this method but it would put most on a more level playing field. By doing this it would allow the people, not the money, to elect the person to office. It would also allow more common citizens of the Republic to run and be elected to political office.

Airwave time could not be purchased but the airwaves should have to donate airwave time of equal amount to each candidate who runs for an office if the airwaves allows any candidate airwave time. The written media would have to do the same. Corporations and other organizations would be allowed to sponsor these time slots so the media would not have to bear a financial burden but each individual would have to have equal time under each time slot.

How would this help? I think it would make for a more fair system for a candidate to run. I think it would get big money out of the picture. I think it would promote more debate type features instead of one candidate standing up there telling everyone how great they are and how terrible the other candidates are just because they have the money to buy air time. I think it would be more informative to the citizens. I think it would get the citizens more involved in the process, as I think they would feel more a part of an election. Most of all, I think it would give control of the government back to the citizens.

Would the elected officials now in office stand for a change of this magnitude? Of course not, as it would erode their power. However, as voting citizens we can force them to accept it as we can boot them out of office every election until we have replaced them with folks who do agree with this method. All it requires from us is to quit thinking along party lines and line up for what is the best for the Republic.

If we don't do something and do it soon the Republic is destined for complete failure. As a nation we are becoming more and more divided each day. Somewhere back in history there was a saying about "Divide and Conquer". Our congress today is so divided down party lines that hardly anything gets accomplished for the good of the nation. The only thing they all readily agree on is any new law that will increase their power and grease their pockets. I thought at one time that when we got women involved some of this would stop but it does not take very long once elected to the house or senate for the ladies to become just as corrupt as the men.

I know a real change is needed. I am not sure how to make that change but I do know that if you don't show up by force as voters the powers to be are not going to worry about 20 to 30% of the population and that's the high side. I know that if not controlled, money is going to continue to be the deciding factor in elections.

That means that corporations, businesses, organizations of all kinds, are going to continue to run the government of the Republic instead of the people. They do not have your best interest at heart. It is up to you to make the change by exerting your power at the ballot box.

Chapter Three
Taxes

    The founding fathers of the Republic did not intend for the citizens to pay individual income taxes. The revenue to run the country was suppose to come from import and export taxes and other commerce where taxes could be collected.

    The first individual income taxes were enacted to pay the cost of the Civil War. I think most citizens can understand that during times like a war a tax may be needed for a period of time to pay for such things. The tax was then appealed somewhere around 1872 and we didn't have an individual income tax again until 1913. The first time the tax was withheld from paychecks was with the 1913 enactment. A lot of controversy surrounded the authority to collect taxes in this manner. Through the next 30 years it was fought over in congress. Then in 1943 the Current Tax

Payment Act was passed by congress and we have been stuck with it every since.

Taxes today are devastating to the average American. The average American gives up almost half of their income in either taxes or fees (another form of taxes) to some government entity. If our taxes were not so high and the way we pay them so wrong we could all enjoy a better life in a more ethical society. The way we are taxed prompts citizens to hide money anyway they can to avoid paying taxes.

The individual income tax should never have been enacted into law. The majority of the citizens did not approve of an individual income tax and they certainly did not want it taken from their paychecks. On the other hand, the government knew taking it in small chunks from the paycheck was about the only way they could collect the tax without causing people to rebel against being taxed. If the citizens were sent a bill at the end of the year and had to fork over the tax in a lump sum they would see how much the tax really hurt. So the government used every means it could muster from cartoons to patriotism to convince congress to pass the 1943 act approving automatic or payroll withholding.

The government's idea was that if a smaller amount was withheld from the paycheck that people would get use to it and not complain and they were right but that doesn't make it right.

Look at how happy people are when they get a refund. Why are they happy? It is their money that the government used for a period of time that they had no opportunity to use to make more money. The government sure doesn't pay you interest for their use but if you are short of deductions and owe a tax they will charge you interest in a heartbeat if you haven't paid in at least 90% for the year.

There are two other reasons that the government pushed for automatic withholding. First, it better insured compliance and second, it allowed the government to access the money year around. If the automatic withholding would not have been enacted many people would not have paid the tax on the due date. At the time the government didn't have in place a very good way to collect if people refused to pay. Hence, the need for the Internal Revenue Service (IRS).

The IRS rewrote due process under the law. They eventually got laws passed that would give them the authority to deny the average citizen the right of due process. If they say you owe taxes they can turn your life into a nightmare. I know they have to be a good collection agency for the government but they should not be allowed the power they have with out due process.

If they claim a person owes taxes the claim should have to go to court where both sides have an opportunity to plead their case. That is not the way it works. If they claim you owe taxes they have the authority to cease all of your property and bank accounts and even your home. Of course this is unconstitutional but they don't care. The burden of proof is then on your back to prove you do not owe the tax. Of course you may not have any means to hire a lawyer but the burden still rest with you. Is this right? I don't think so.

In the recent years, after hearing years of complaints from citizens that had been black booted by the IRS, congress passed some reforms that asks for a gentler IRS. I hope this will become policy. However, our tax system is the reason the IRS is even needed.

One of the reasons our taxes are so high is due to government policies. Our import/export tax system is so far out of whack that we citizens have to make up revenue that the government should be collecting in import taxes. When goods are shipped overseas the countries where they are shipped charge us very high import taxes. On the other hand, when goods are shipped into the Republic from other countries that directly compete with our goods they do not have to pay an equally high import tax. This allows goods coming into the Republic to be sold at a lower price than the goods produced in the Republic.

Ray Reeves

We also have other ways we beat ourselves on import taxes. We allow a lot lower import tax if part of the product being imported is assembled in the Republic. For example, Let's say a pickup truck is imported from China. If that truck comes in fully assembled a higher import tax is placed on it. If it comes in with the tailgate not attached then the import tax is much less because some U.S. worker will be paid to attach the tailgate. The importing country gets hundreds of dollars in import tax savings and the U.S. worker that assembled it may have been earning $15.00 an hour. It would probably take the worker ten minutes to install the tailgate. The other countries do not allow this in their countries. This puts the U.S. at a great disadvantage.

We have a very large balance of payment debt in the Republic and a system such as above is one of the reasons. When we export something such as an automobile to another country an import tax is placed on it that is so high that most people in that country cannot afford to buy it so they buy one of their own makes. When you reverse that and their automobile is sent over here we charge them a low import tax, which allows them to sell their automobile cheaper than our manufacturers can sell ours so the citizen buys the imported automobile.

Fortunately, in the past few years a lot of foreign automobile manufacturers have set up plants in the Republic allowing our workers to benefit from earning wages. The Republic gains from the taxes the workers pay and it is a lot better for everyone. The automobile industry is about the only industry that has done that on any large scale so most of the other industries are under the other system.

In my opinion there are viable solutions to the many tax problems we have in the Republic that is strangling the average citizen and hurting the poor very much also. I am not real concerned with the rich in one sense, as they do not pay out as great of a percentage of their income as does the average citizen.

Let us begin with the Individual Income Tax. I think it should be abolished yesterday. This tax is so unfair to most average citizens as to their ability to have loopholes that the poor and the rich have. Let's say the average worker earns $30,000.00 per year. In order to fill out a long form so you can have deductions you must have a minimum base amount of deductible items. I think that amount in 2003 was $9500.00. Forgive me if I am wrong but it really doesn't matter that much as an example anyway. So the worker must come up with at least $9500.00 in deductions before they can use the long form to figure their taxes. Unless they have had a very high medical expense during the year about the only other thing the IRS allows is mortgage interest and real estate taxes. That means that their interest payments on the mortgage would have to be about $790.00 a month. The mortgage payment would probably have to be around $1000.00 per month. Most workers would not qualify for a mortgage of this size based on their income. That means that they would have to have two incomes to qualify for a large enough mortgage to start taking deductions for other things such as medical insurance, donations, real estate taxes, etc. If you have a combined family income using the average you are now looking at paying taxes on $60,000.00 per year which puts you in a higher bracket. Also, all the expenses that are not deductible are doubled as you now need two cars, day care if children are involved, twice as much for food, clothes, and on and on. Consequently, most in the $30,000.00 dollar wage range has little choice except to pay the top amount of taxes.

Compare this to the rich who can afford and qualify for the mortgage that will far surpass the $9500.00 base. They can easily use the allowed deductions bringing their earned income down to a level that they can easily afford compared to the average worker's income. They all have ways to avoid taxes and still be able to live a very nice life style in a very nice home and send their children to very nice schools and probably pay less individual income taxes, as did the average worker. For certain they will pay out a lower percentage of their income than the average worker will.

Then when you consider the poor they may or may not pay out as high of a percentage as the average worker depending on individual cases. If the poor have children they usually qualify for a credit that will allow a $3000.00 refund and they may not have paid in a penny. I don't necessarily begrudge them the little help they get from the rest of the taxpayers but in so many cases the poor are poor due to their own making. I think you can probably read between the lines here to know what I mean without spelling it out.

My offered solution is either a flat tax or a consumption tax. In case you are not familiar with either or both of these I will try to briefly explain as I understand them. The flat tax is basically what it sounds like. A tax of a specific percentage that all income levels pay at the same rate. One of the proposals that I have heard about is 15%. This tax would probably be somewhat fair if a standard amount for everyone was not subject to the tax. For the purpose of this example let's say no one is taxed on the first $10,000.00 of income. After that no other deductions would be allowed. So if the poor worker earned $18,000.00 a year they would only have to pay taxes on $8000.00 dollars at 15% or $1200.00 dollars. The average worker would have to pay 15% of $20,000 after the standard $10,000.00 is deducted for an annual tax burden of $3000.00. That is probably about what they pay now but it would be so much simpler and they would know what the tax burden was going to be before the end of the year and could better budget the remaining income. The rich, and I am going to use $125,000.00 as a base here, would get the $10,000.00 deduction and pay 15% percent of the remaining $115,000.00 or $17,250.00. This would mean that the poor worker paid in approximately 7% of income in taxes, the average worker paid in approximately 10% of his income and the rich worker paid in approximately 15% of his income. You can see the rich fairs a lot better than the others when you consider how much money they still have to spend.

The thing I dislike most about the flat tax is that it would leave all the other taxes in place. You would still have to pay a flat amount plus still be faced with all the other sales taxes, gas taxes, excise taxes, real estate taxes, etc. The flat tax is an income tax only.

The tax system that I would best like to defend is the consumption tax. I am not sure I fully understand it but I think I may have a fairly good handle on the way it works. The consumption tax is somewhat similar for the average citizen that I experienced in Germany many years ago. I have no idea what they use there now and really do not care, as it is not important to our situation here in the U.S.

The way the consumption tax works with business and manufacturing can get complicated as they pay the tax at different stages of the enterprise so I will not dwell on that part of the tax. It is quite simple for the individual. Basically, all other taxes, with the exception of the social security tax would no longer exist, as we know them now. There would be no individual income tax. Some fees would probably still be a possibility.

As a citizen living your everyday life you would pay a set amount on everything you purchased or any service you obtained. For this example let us use the figure of 20%. If you bought a hamburger and a shake that cost $3.00 then you would pay $3.60. The .60 cents would be divided among all the taxing authorities. You or I would not have anymore to do with it after we had paid. Some agency, probably a state agency, would have the task of dividing it. If you bought a gallon of gas at a cost of $1.50 a consumption tax of .30 cents would be added at the pump and your cost would be $1.80. If you bought a pair of shoes for the price of $25.00 you would pay an additional consumption tax of $5.00 and so on. If you get a haircut for $10.00 it would cost you $12.00.

This may sound high and 20% may not be the actual figure needed but the advantages of this system would be so easy to live with. Don't forget no other taxes would be necessary so the IRS would no longer be needed saving the government billions of dollars a year. If you were a homeowner you would no longer pay school taxes, as they would get a share of the 20%.

In this manner everyone would pay the same amount of tax based on how much they spend. This would allow the individual to determine how much of their income they wanted to pay out in taxes by how much they spend. If you are rich and want to drive a Mercedes then you would pay the 20% tax when you bought the automobile. If you are satisfied with a Ford Focus then you will save a lot more on taxes than the person who bought the Mercedes. Another great feature of this is that the tax can be added to the price of an item allowing the consumer to see the full cost of an item. If you seen an article of clothing in the store window priced at $32.50 you would know that would be the total cost.

Presently we pay a whole lot more than 20% of our income in taxes. If you own a home you pay even more than non-homeowners do and since owning a home is an American dream most of us either own or will someday own a home. Consider all the taxes the average person pays and it will approach the 40% or higher rate. A short list that many of us pay is: Individual Income Tax

Sales Tax

Real Estate Tax (included are school taxes)

Social Security Tax

Gasoline Tax

Tobacco Tax (for the ones who use)

Excise Tax

Luxury Tax

Inspection Sticker fees

Building permit fees

Registration fees

Dog tags

Cell phone taxes

Home phone tax

Long distance tax

and it goes on and on and every time a government entity wants more revenue they just pass another tax or fee or increase the ones in place and we have no choice except to pay it.

We will probably never see a fair tax as the wealthy does not want to pay their fare share and they are the ones we send to congress year after year to make the laws. If we ever do have a fair change in the way we are taxed it will have to come from a widely accepted change that the people will demand the government to accept and enact.

Since Russia has become a democratic country they have enacted a flat tax and their economy is booming. The people do not mind paying out 15% as they realize the government needs funds to run the government, build infrastructure, provide for national security, and health care. They have very little tax cheating by the average citizen hiding income. Don't get me wrong, I would much rather pay a larger tax and live in this country but the point here is that we should not have to pay the larger tax. If a country like Russia can create a tax that is more fair to the average citizen then we should be able to also create a fairer tax.

It would not be easy, as congress and the rich (who actually run congress) will object and it would take a unified effort but I believe we can force the congress to quit robbing us with taxes. Compare the 20% tax to the present system using the example of the $30,000.00 average worker. If they spent every penny they earned through the year their tax would be $6000.00. Presently if you add all the taxes and fees paid on the $30,000.00 it will exceed 30% and probably reach 40 % or as much as $12,000.00. Which would you rather pay? It is your money and you should care.

Chapter Four
New World Order

The New World Order is not new, nor is it order. It is a vision of the very elite wealthy of the world, mostly European to dominate the world through the use of the United Nations and the banks owned by the wealthy. You say, tell me the names and prove your theory. Well, I cannot do that for several reasons. One of the best reasons was what I wrote in the Foreword about being lazy. You or I could do the research if we cared enough. The truth is there but in many cases is well hidden. I have done enough research to satisfy my opinion. If you did want to research what I write you can start with the name of Bilderberg. My purpose in this chapter is not to prove what I say but instead it is to inform those of you who may care that this does exist.

You see, the very wealthy of the world does not give a hoot about anyone in this world that is not in their circle. The average person to them is like a worker bee. You work to support the queen and the hive but you are very dispensable. There are a lot of wealthy in today's world that is not in that circle, as their money is not the old world money, but in most cases they would be welcome to join the elite if they have the same vision. Some of those who would fit into that category have voiced that the world is too populated, owns a vast amount of land, and donates money to the UN. Does this over population attitude reflect the possibility that mass murder throughout the world would be acceptable? Do not ever doubt that, as evil exists with power and the ultra wealthy have power. Why should they allow more people on earth than is necessary to do their daily bidding? After all, why use up the natural resources on unnecessary humans?

We common everyday people and the poor of the world can not even imagine the amount of wealth there is in the world held by a relative few (compared to world population) families. Many of these families are of European decent. Many are descendents of European families going back to the Middle Ages and perhaps even farther back. Many are of Royalty from the ages when Kings and Queens were a lot more numerous than now.

For centuries they have plotted and planned how to bring about a world in which they are the supreme masters and the rest of the world's people are slaves unto them, of course slave here is not literal, as in leg irons and chains. The world being as large as it is now and as diverse as it is now has complicated their dreams and visions. Some have even had to drop out of the circle due to loss of wealth.

This vision for a New World Order is basically the same as The One World Order that is a name that may be better known. Many events in history were the result of manipulation by the planners of the Order. Check out WWI, I think you may find some clues there, as to how wealth and power can motivate. They are not obvious, as much of it must be held in secret to preserve the vision until the day that it can be implemented. This isn't going to happen overnight. It has been in progress for a long time but our time, as a free people in a freedom-loving nation is rapidly coming to an end. I predict that by 2050 or sooner the New World Order will be in place or just around the corner. You say, "So What", I won't be around to see it. What about your children and grandchildren do you not care what happens to them?

I will tell you one place that does have a lot of information on the subject but I will leave it up to you to do your own research, believe what you want from the sources, and do what you will with the information you find. The web sight that has a lot of information is "InfoWars.Com". This web site has a lot of links to other sites that also have information.

One of the events that have played very effectively into the plan is the founding of the United Nations (UN). I do not know how much the New World Order elite had to do with the forming of the UN but I would suspect a lot. I say this as it fits so perfectly into the plan.

I consider the UN a very important part of the New World Order plans, actually, it is a vital link in the Order. Without the UN or something very similar the New World Order cannot and will not happen. I must write a little about the way I feel about the UN based on the research I have done and my gut feelings. Sometimes trusting your intuitions will be a better guide than propaganda written about a subject.

The original founding of the UN sounded pretty good and it was an easy sell. WWII had just ended and the world was tired of war. The UN was envisioned to bring nations together to try and prevent future wars as well as promote other social ideas. As with many organizations the good intentions are later manipulated and refined into something far from the original purpose. This is what has happened with the UN.

Today the main goal of the UN is not to prevent war and help underprivileged nations but instead it has evolved into an organization hell bent on running the world. The elite who want the New World Order has encouraged this. The UN is going to be their enforcer of laws for the Order. Once it is in place any country that causes problems including the present permanent members of the security council will find UN forces on their soil enforcing UN laws in a martial law type atmosphere. No nation will have sovereignty, as we know it today.

Oh yes, the UN charter sounds real sweet and dreamy on the surface and in many ways is similar to our constitution. It has a bill of rights, of sorts, and everything. Where the greatest difference is and should matter to every citizen of the Republic is in the Judicial. When the New World Order becomes a reality you and I will no longer have a right to due process that we now enjoy. You will be tried in UN courts and World courts. Some members of your present Supreme Court who are suppose to be protecting the constitution of the Republic agree that this might not be a bad idea. This is really scary. You may have noticed I used "When" earlier, it is going to happen unless you help prevent it from happening by demanding that we get out of the UN. I really think that if the United States would pull out of the UN it would collapse within two years. We could then start a new organization that would restrict membership to nations who believe in freedom and cannot be manipulated by the wealthy.

Today the UN is made up of about 191 member nations. There are a few countries that are not members. Things such as the break up of the USSR can change the number of members that make up the UN but for now I think the actual number is 191. Most of these nations are not like the major nations such as the European nations, the United States, Russia, China, (China is included here because of its impact on the world in the future) etc. Many are poor nations ran by dictators that could care less about their citizens. Many are not of the democratic persuasion and some are controlled by religious zealots. In addition, there are thousands of organizations that are recognized as supporters of the UN and they receive special recognition in the UN. These are not the type of countries I want dictating how we run our country or making laws that affect me or my family. They are also not the types of people I want judging any citizen of the Republic in UN courts.

Many of these other nations who do not enjoy the freedoms that most of us still enjoy here cannot be allowed to judge our way of life. They cannot be allowed to continue dictating to the Republic what we can and cannot do with our national treasures. How many of you know that we as a sovereign country must have UN approval before doing certain things in Yellowstone National Park and the Grand Canyon National Park. Why? Because the UN claim that they are World Treasures and our leaders allowed the UN to have a say in what is done in the parks. These kinds of things are happening all over the world. Did you know the UN is trying to get the authority to place a tax on you and me to help support the UN? Some of this tax will eventually end up in the hands of dictators. Is that where you want your money to go?

The United States pays the largest amount to support the UN. Good luck if you try to find the total amount. It is like the CIA budget. No one seems to know the exact amount. I am betting that it is in the billions. In addition, we house the UN in New York where the diplomats from other countries run amuck in violating our laws because they have diplomatic immunity. This immunity extends to anywhere they wish to travel in the U.S. They park where they please and it is useless for the police to issue parking tickets, as they are never paid. They speed over our roads without fear of consequences. Many may be involved in smuggling, as their diplomatic pouches cannot be searched. If they get in trouble by committing a felonious crime about the most that will happen to them is that they will be asked to leave the U.S.

Because the elite who plan for a New World Order are the ones who control the money of the world through the banks they own they will actually be the ones in charge of the UN. They will dictate to the UN what they want accomplished, when they want it accomplished, and how they want it accomplished. If that means the use of force the UN forces will be used to arrive at the desired objective. This will be accomplished because no nation will have the ability to resist, as one of the main objectives of the UN is world disarmament. The UN will control the only arms.

One of the stumbling blocks facing the New World Order is the fact that so many citizens of so many countries are still armed. The United States citizens are the best armed. It was a deterrent to Japan during WWII to keep them from invading the U.S. They simply did not know how they could defeat a country whose citizens were so well armed. It is still a deterrent to, a take over by force, the New World Order advocate's still have to overcome. However, they are doing it one step at a time. There is no real urgency and patience is one thing they have. Remember that this New World Order vision is centuries old. That is one reason why it is so very important that this Republic's citizens retain the right to bear arms. Many countries have already given up this right. Then there are others like Switzerland who make it mandatory that all the males citizens between certain ages have military training and maintain a government issued weapon in their homes. This is a really great idea. When was the last time they were ever attacked? Hitler even decided it would not be feasible.

There are many advocates for a New World Order running the Republic today. Look at where many of your representatives and senators stand on the issue and you may be shocked. These are people that we citizens have voted into office to represent our interest and they swear an oath to uphold The Constitution of the United States of America. The last time I read the constitution I did not see anyplace in it where the UN or a New World Order was mentioned.

I know some of you may think a system controlling the world such as the UN would be a good thing. I know that in our public schools and everywhere else there is a forum that our children are being taught this and how great the world would be if there was peace everywhere and all peoples had plenty to eat and shelter from the elements. I would also like to see a world where no child went to bed hungry and no child would lose their arms and legs by some radical that gives life no value. However, it is never going to happen, not in ten years, not in a hundred years, not in a thousand years. It will not happen in a New World Order. It cannot happen because of language and religious differences in the world.

When two people or a thousand people do not speak the same language and have different religious beliefs they are never going to live side by side in complete harmony. Having a world religion is part of the plan the New World Order zealots want. It would not necessarily be a religion about God but may be spiritual in love of the earth, environment, and mankind. They realize that a common religious or spiritual belief is necessary if unity is to be a reality.

If our Republic allows a New World Order to evolve the Republic with all of its opportunities and freedoms will cease to exist. Some of our leaders want the New World Order, as they believe they will be part of the elite that will rule the world. I would not bet on that happening. Be careful when you go vote. Be careful of the credentials they have such as being a Rhodes Scholar. The Rhodes Scholars are taught that they and only they are qualified to properly rule the world. Most of us just know them as being very smart but they are indoctrinated in the New World Order.

Two very important steps to the New World order are already in place in the UN. One is the World Trade Organization and the other is the International Monetary Fund. These are designed to regulate trade throughout the world and to control what nations will receive funds through the UN. The UN also wants a world money system that has UN money instead of each nation having their own. When that happens our money may not be worth half as much as it is now. So when you are forced to exchange dollars for UN money you may only receive half or even less than the present value in dollars. A first step to this is the recent Euro currency introduced in Europe. Our dollar got a hit against the euro to boost the value of the euro. Remember those wanting a New World Order own most of the largest banks in the world. Who do you think is going to be in control of the UN money?

You may say, "What about the Federal Reserve", since they are in charge of our money now. If you ask this question then you need to learn about the Federal Reserve, that is neither Federal nor a Reserve. It is in fact, the same banks that I have been writing about controlled by the same families who want the New World Order.

I think we can leave the UN and bring with us the countries that would be most beneficial to our way of life. We do not need a bunch of countries controlled by dictators and religious fanatics sucking the blood out of our veins. The Republic can stand forever if the citizens will stand up to protect what it stands for and that my friend is "Freedom".

I mentioned China earlier and I want to expand a little on that and say that China could be our salvation in there ever being a One-World Government. They are rapidly becoming a more capitalistic style of country. This may or may not make them more democratic in their views but I think it will. Their economy is growing by leaps and bounds. They have over one sixth of the world population. They are a nuclear power. They have the largest standing military in the world and overnight can have millions more in the military. I have my doubts that they will ever go along with the one world government as I think they will always want to maintain their sovereignty. I don't think they will allow the UN to dictate policy to them.

Footnote: If you are interested in learning more about UN plans I would recommend reading "The United Nations Welfare Giveaway" by Cliff Kincaid. He is the President of American Survival, Inc. The book comes in paperback, is easy to read, and is about 100 pages long. If you have doubts about the UN intentions this book may open your eyes a little. *ISBN 0-9704070-0-9*

Chapter Five
<u>Race Relations</u>

I have a dream, I have a dream that someday all the people of this great country can live a life where it is not necessary to refer to themselves as a type of American. I dream of a time when every citizen can simply say, "I am an American". It is not important to me if you are an African American, a Hispanic American, a Native American, an Irish American, an Asian American or any other ethnic nationality. These ethnic names in front of American are one of the things that keep us divided. It separates us into categories. The only title I care about in front of American is Loyal.

I guess we all have our thoughts and opinions about the different races that make up our country. My views have changed some over the years as I have learned more and been exposed to many different races. I have, and will probably always have, bad feelings toward **individuals** of all races and ethnic backgrounds but I try very hard not to ever blame a race on my feelings toward an **individual**, as that is not a fair way. **Individual** actions that I do not personally approve of by any **individual** will cause me disgust toward that **individual** no matter what the race or ethnic background. There are some races that I do not trust. This is probably because I don't know them very well. I don't think I am alone in this.

This chapter will have a lot more about Blacks than other races. I will refer to the African American race as Black, as this seems to be acceptable to them for the most part. Using African American each time I refer to them would be tedious, as in my first paragraph I mentioned that I really do not like the division of Americans by ethnic background. I can understand why they may not like to be referred to as Negro or as Colored. Both of these titles are associated too closely with slavery. The reason I will write mostly about Blacks is because other than the Native Americans I think Blacks have had a raw deal for the most part in this country until 1964 and it should not have been that way for almost 400 years. They should not have had to wait 100 years and it takes an act of congress for their freedoms to be protected. They have been here almost as long as the White founders and they have done much to build this nation. No other race, other than Europeans, has immigrated to this country, whether by chance or choice, longer ago than the Blacks. I am excluding the Spanish explorers as most did not stay in this country as residents and builders of the nation, instead they came to plunder.

I was pretty lucky growing up not to have had a father and mother that was prejudice to the point that they taught their children to hate because of race. That gave my brothers and sisters and me a leg up on so many others who had just the opposite type of parents. I am not real sure why my Dad had the views about race that he had but I think it was because he was raised dirt poor and pulled cotton right along side those of other races and came to know them and the plight they all suffered together.

I had a friend of my own race growing up and he would get whippings if his Dad even heard he had talked to a Black person. I only know of one incident where that happened but it shows how much some hate other races and how they teach their children that hate. That friend had to have grown up with the same hatred even as unfounded as it was. I hope he has changed by now. Of course this didn't bother my relationship with the friend, I just felt sorry for him.

My Dad usually worked in places where there would be at least one black man and as far back, as I can remember they were always friends. Of course we children always liked these friends of Dad and it was not until I was older that the race issue even became apparent in my life. Except for Dad's friends I was really not exposed to another race until I was in junior high. Junior high school was the first time that I can remember ever going to school with Black students. Even then there were not very many. I went to high school in the same town and the high school was also integrated and this was in the middle 50s.

I can not remember any serious incidents over race at our school. I think there was a small incident at one time about a white girl dating a black guy but it never came close to getting out of hand. We had some Blacks and Hispanics on the football and basketball teams that enhanced our teams winning ability. It was like most of us just accepted the fact that they were part of the school. I am sure there was some animosity by some toward the Blacks and the Hispanics but I don't remember others talking about the issue of going to school with either. After school we all went our separate ways.

After high school I joined the military and of course in 1959 the military was already integrated but it was nothing new to me. In the military we were exposed to classes in Race Relations (hence, where I got the title for this chapter). These classes were intended for us to learn more about other races and ethnic backgrounds. I believe it helped many of us have a better understanding of others. One thing about the Air Force was that they would not tolerate displays of racial conflicts between members. I am sure this was a deterrent to some who otherwise may not have been tolerant of each other.

Since I had gone to school with Blacks for several years and I had been in the military for a while I was kind of surprised to see the remnants of segregation in 1960 while hitchhiking from Hobbs, New Mexico to San Antonio, Texas. In Lamesa, Texas they still had segregated restrooms and water fountains at the bus station. The only other time I saw anything of this nature was in the South in the middle to late 60s.

Yes, I am guilty of using the N-word at different times and I think most of us have used it at sometime in our lives, especially if we are over 50. However, I can't ever remember using it in any face to face encounter when I was angry with the person. Being White and being in the presence of other Whites I have told jokes where the N-word embellished the joke. I am sure most Blacks in the same age group have used Whitey or Cracker when they told jokes about whites within their own circle of friends. It doesn't make it right from either side but it is just something that happens. Today's stand up comics use ethnic names and slang all the time to embellish their routine. Many of us are tolerant of things that we know are meant to make us laugh and not to make us angry. I try now to not even tell jokes that disrespects other races but occasional I still do. I would much rather disrespect a politician and I assure you they deserve the disrespect in most cases. As a matter of fact, a political person can often times replace a race in a joke and it will be just as funny and to some of us who basically dislike politicians it may be funnier.

While in the military I had some friends or at least I considered them friends and I think they generally felt the same toward me that were of other races. Most of them I liked just as much as my White friends. Some of them I have missed after transfers, more or less, ended our friendships. You might ask why didn't I keep in touch with them. Well, many times I wish that I had. But then, I have not kept in touch with very many of my White friends either. It is just the way I am.

One of those friends was Walter Hutchens (it may have been Hutchenson but 40 plus years dims the memory). We all just called him Hutch. He was in the army and even though I was in the air force we were both cooks and because the air force dining hall fed a lot of the army troops he was assigned to our dining hall. Hutch was probably close to 40 when I knew him. He was a Staff Sergeant if I remember correctly. I was

19 and an A2/C so we had nothing in common as far as service branches, age, or rank, but we became friends.

Hutch grew up in Georgia and he use to tell me how things were growing up as a Black kid in Georgia. He use to tell me how he would frequently be jumped and beat up by White kids. He told me that being spit on was an everyday occurrence and there was little he could do about it, as in Georgia in the 20s and 30s when he grew up there they would still lynch a Black person for protecting himself against attacks by Whites. It is hard for me to imagine why there was such cruelty towards another human being just because of a skin color. The White people that would do something like that had to be taught that type of hatred and conduct at home.

Hutch was such a great guy and I use to love to talk with him. He use to loan me his 56 pink and white Cadillac and I would drive it up to Frankfurt and flirt with the fraulines. After I retired and got my first computer I did try to find Hutch. I would love to see him again. I imagine by now and even years ago when I tried to find him that he may have already passed.

I wonder why there is so much hatred toward the Black race. They have done so much to build this nation and it is not any Black's fault, living or dead, that they are here. The Indians were smart when slavery first started in this country. When the white man would try to make slaves out of the Indians they would just wait for the first chance they had and escape back into the woods and they could not be found. The Blacks could not do this, as everyone knew if you were Black then you were a slave and they were always returned. This was not always true, especially later, as some Blacks were free but it was a general view of Blacks until the end of slavery.

Blacks built the huge agriculture industry in this country from the north to the south. Of course they did not have a choice but never the less it was their labor, sweat, and tears, that accomplished the feat. There would not have been the large plantations in the south if not for the Black labor.

Many of you may not know that Black slave labor built the original Washington DC. Isn't that so ironic? A nation founded on freedom yet the nations capitol was built by slaves. The main reason the site where Washington DC was originally laid out was that it was close to the two states that had the largest slave population, Virginia and Maryland. If I remember my history correctly the land was donated by ole George himself who also owned slaves.

Another thing that I think is ironic is that the nation was suppose to be so religious but yet they used religion to help justify slavery. Some used the story of Noah and Cannan to justify slavery. I don't personally know the story but it had something to do with Noah putting a curse on Cannan that he would be a slave. That may have extended from the mark God was supposed to have put on Cain for killing Able, as some believe the mark was a black skin. On the other hand, the first abolitionist, The Quakers, used religion to show where slavery was wrong. For many years slaves were not allowed to practice a religion. Later it was decided that it might be a good idea for them to be Christians. This may have been strange to the ones who had practiced a religion in Africa as many tribes in Africa practiced paganism and perhaps a form of Islam. However, church became very important to slaves as it allowed some socializing and gave them a common thread. Church is still very important to many Blacks. Fortunately, they can now attend integrated churches if they so desire. There are some that I think use religion as a front for their own financial gain but then I also think this about a lot of Whites.

Integration has finally made great strides since 1964. I think this is good for the country. It has allowed a great many Whites to rethink the myths about Blacks being inferior to Whites. When Blacks are given the opportunity and take advantage of the opportunity to become educated they are very much on the equal with all races. You can take any race and if they do not have an opportunity for education they will be inferior, intelligence wise, to anyone who has more education. The problem some Blacks have is that they won't take advantage of the educational opportunities they have, however, they are not alone in this. Many other races will not take advantage either including the White race. I know some pretty dumb Whites.

I think I can somewhat understand why Blacks were considered inferior back when they were abducted in Africa to be brought to the colonies. The life style many of them lived in Africa in the 17th century was such that they really did not need much of a formal education. Most lived in tribes that were hunters and gathers so most of what they needed to know was how to kill game and know what plants were safe to eat. On the other hand, European Whites were somewhat educated, especially compared to Blacks. There was also a great language bearer. So when Blacks were first introduced as slaves in the colonies they may have seemed really stupid to the Whites. After all, they did not even know farming. But probably even more important is the fact that they were not even treated as human.

If I had been a Black slave in the 17th century I would have been full of resentment for being forced into slavery and I would have resisted as much as possible short of being beat. So I suspect that White owners also had attitudes to deal with. All during the days of slavery they never had an opportunity to show just how intelligence they could be with the proper education.

Today we have Blacks that have made great contributions to this country going back at least as far as George Washington Carver. If you do not know how much Dr. Carver contributed to agriculture then you may be somewhat inferior yourself. He was also an accomplished musician and artist.

Very few had the opportunity before that to make contributions except the ones used as slave labor to build the Capitol and the soldiers who fought as Federal troops in the Civil War. Since then there has been many great Blacks. Some took up arms to fight for their own freedom and many have taken up arms since to defend what we stand for as a nation. Blacks become just as good of a soldier and airman as any other race. Again, they had a lot of restrictions placed on them in the military until the military was finally integrated in 1948. But even with that, Blacks and other units made up of minorities before integration excelled as solders and airmen.

I am glad that I was not raised in the south where the hatred for Blacks was so perverse. I am glad that they are finally coming around to accept Blacks as fellow Americans. There is still a lot of hatred in the south, and the north for that matter, but at least Blacks are protected by laws now that are usually enforced instead of ignored.

Affirmative Action has kept the hatred alive to a large extent but I think for the time that it has been in place that it has helped the Blacks at least get a foot hold on the ladder of fairness. I have personally been affected by affirmative action when looking for jobs but when I was told I could not be hired because the firm or company did not have enough minorities working then I just went to another place of employment where I could be hired. Many employers used the excuse that they could not find qualified Blacks to fill jobs but more often than not they would not hire them and train them so they could become qualified. However, now I pretty much favor doing away with the affirmative action quotas as I think now it may be doing almost as much harm as good. Many will disagree with that but affirmative action like welfare somewhat takes away dignity from people.

I believe that welfare caused most of the problems the Blacks have had over the past 50 years. The problems I refer to are the number of families where the father was not in the picture, as in many cases that could stop a family from qualifying for welfare and this caused many children to grow up without fathers. In other cases it caused the women to have multiple births, as the more children a woman had the larger welfare check she received. I realize the powers to be had good intentions with welfare but again it is a system that takes a persons dignity away and in some ways makes them a lesser person dependent on handouts. I don't think most people can think much of themselves or have much confidence to go out and improve their lives under those conditions.

One of the other bad aspects that welfare caused was that the rent subsidies that usually went along with welfare was the main reason that caused the ghettos in the larger cities. Living in a ghetto I am sure took most of a persons hopes away. I never lived in a ghetto and the only thing I have to base my opinion on is the depictions of ghettos on TV and in movies. It must be a terrible place to raise children or to live period. Children that do want to better their lives have so many obstacles to overcome that it is almost impossible to breakout. Many Black males in the period during welfare at least until 1964 who lived in the ghetto usually had a police record by the time they reached 21. It is double hard to get a job with a criminal record as without. That caused many of them to make money by way of crime. Consequently, many of the Black males ended up in prison with their lives basically ruined.

If you look at the Black men who grew up in places other than the ghetto you will find a lot greater percentage that did and does well in life. We may have to exclude the south in this until after 1964. Most Blacks want the same kind of life as most Whites or other races want. It has been and still is a lot harder for that to happen if you are Black. I have had the good fortune to know some Black families that have made good and have made it even better for their children by making sure they got a good education. Of course they did not have it easy and had to work very hard many times for less pay than what their White co-workers earned for the same job. We are seeing more and more success stories everyday.

Several things have always bothered me about so many black males. It seems to me that with all the imprisonment as slaves that their forefathers experienced that the last thing they would want is to continue living a slave life behind prison bars. Being behind bars most of your life must not be much better than being a slave. Oh sure, you may eat better, and in today's world you have TV to watch and can make phone calls, can have visitors, and get to go to the yard for recreation, probably no beatings, but you have no real freedom. Yet, even with the opportunities they have today so many of them continue to do criminal acts that either get them killed or they end up in prison. Much of the time the criminal acts is perpetrated against his own people. It just doesn't make sense to me.

Another thing that is hard for me to understand is how they can produce children with so many different women and never offer any responsibility toward raising the children. Can they not realize that the children really need a father figure to help them become responsible citizens or do they just not care, as so many of them were raised without fathers. Now you and I both know that it is not all of them by any means but there is a large percentage compared to what there should be. In addition, many of them belong to gangs that terrorize their own neighborhoods, sell drugs to children, pimp their prostitutes, kill innocent by-standers in gang related drive-by shootings and many other criminal acts. I am not implying that only Black males do these things but the percentages are very high in their race.

Do Blacks deserve reparations? I have several viewpoints on this subject. I think it is late in the season for a harvest of this nature. The freed Blacks were originally promised 40 acres and a mule. This was never paid. It should have been. I think two other options were available in 1865. One of them would not have been practical and one of them would not have been fair. If the promise of the 40 acres and a mule was not going to be honored then I think the next thing should have been done. That would have been to take

Georgia, Alabama, and Florida and make a Black America and deported all the Blacks to their own country.

The United States and Black America would have been like any other foreign countries doing commerce together. Import and export taxes, passports, and similar would have been necessary for visitation and or commerce. As this doesn't even begin to sound logical it could not have been done.

The other thing would have been to load all the Blacks on ships and send them back to Africa. How fair would that have been? None of the original slaves would even have been alive. All that were here in 1865 were born here and that automatically made them United States Citizens. None of them would have spoken the African languages and probably would not have been welcomed back either.

None of our Black citizens today suffered any of the personal pain of slavery. However, I would consider reparations on limited bases provided that the Native Americans would also receive reparations for the harms we did to them. The bases I would consider would be to all descendents of slaves who were still in slavery at the end of the Civil War, and factual proof would be required. From these the following should be eliminated: Any descendant that received welfare for more than five years and any descendant that committed a felony and served over five years in prison. I hope you can understand my logic here.

Now what should the reparation be? I think anyone over the age of 40 should receive $50,000.00 tax-free (which would be equivalent to several hundred thousand and maybe even a million in the slave days). It is much more difficult to go to college after age 40 than under 40 and that is why they should have the cash option. If they want to use it for college that would be their decision. Anyone under 40 would have free tuition at a state college in their home state for five years to include books and fees. How do I arrive at these conclusions? Blacks over 40 in most cases were still denied many opportunities prior to 1964. I think $50,000.00 would be a fair amount for doing nothing except being a qualified recipient. Especially, since they have absolutely nothing in the way of reparation now. Those under 40 have pretty much had many of the same opportunities as many Whites have had, as the civil rights act is 40 this year. By paying for their tuition they would be gaining a free education that should allow them equal opportunity in the future and they would not blow a set amount of money foolishly.

How would it be funded? Simply by adding a 10% tax on all legal gambling and a 5% additional tax on corporations conducting business outside of the United States. Then listen to all the crybabies. I feel sorry for neither as one makes large profits and the other has sent many jobs out of this country that Blacks and Whites could be holding down.

I think our country is lucky to have our diversity in so many areas of our daily lives. Just think of all the sports where Blacks have made the games so exciting. Think of all of the great music that we would not have if not for Black artist. Think about some of the great movies we have enjoyed with great performances by the Black stars. Think about the greatest stars of all, the Blacks who are willing to give their lives and those who did give their lives defending this country that they love and is their home too. They deserve to eat at the same table with the rest of the family of Americans and be treated as equals.

I know we have the other races that have made many contributions to the Republic also but for some reason it seems the Hispanic and Asians have been a lot more readily accepted into our society than Blacks. I know there are areas where there are problems. However, it hasn't seemed to divide us, as has the Black issue.

I think there is a possibility that the illegal immigrant issue may cause us some serious problems some day. However, this can be stopped in its tracks by the government enforcing the laws already on the books. All we need is an administration with the guts to enforce the law and not let it slide so their cronies can continue to have cheap but exploited labor.

As a country and as a society I think it is high time we put the past behind us and move on as a nation. The ones who spend their lives trying to keep us divided should be told to set down, shut up, and if you don't like things here then get the hell out. They know who they are and I think you do too.

Chapter Six
<u>Religion</u>

This chapter will probably get me in trouble with my friends and family, as most of them are pretty religious. If I offend them and they are truly Christians then they should be able to forgive me, accept me, and remain friends. I also expect the same from my family. If they no longer want to be my friend that will be their choice but it will give me a lot better insight as to their real Christian views, as I understand Christianity.

I think those of you who have the faith it takes to believe in God are more fortunate than those of us who do not. Many of us live each day searching for the answer. Hoping to hear something or see something that will give us the proof we need in order to believe. We have no one to turn to for comfort when we are down or depressed. We are made to feel guilty in the presence of those who believe. It would be a much easier life if we could just accept what we have been told all of our lives but for some of us we must have proof. Faith is just not enough.

I do not know a lot about any religion and to many this may cause you to think that it is not something I should write about. This may be a valid point if I was trying to convince you of something specific. However, this is not my intent. I believe I have enough knowledge to form my opinions of why I have my doubts of a Christian God and him as the creator of all life. Since I have my most knowledge in the Christian religion and this was where I was indoctrinated as a child I will write mostly of things that affect my Christian non-beliefs and doubts.

I just cannot find the faith it takes to be a Christian. There are just too many things that do not add up in the Christian doctrine. There are too many conflicts and contradictions in the Bible in my opinion. My personality makes me too weak to have the faith required to accept Christianity based on my view of the facts and what I see in the real world. I have to admit that it may be possible that a supreme power created what we know as the universe, however, it is very difficult for me to believe it was the Christian God of the Bible. Scientific proof of evolution is also lacking; however, faith in science is not required to accept scientific facts and theories.

I do not really care how others label me. You can call me an Atheist, an Agnostic, a non-believer, or any other term you care to use. I prefer to be considered as a Doubter where religion is concerned.

The one thing that I am not is a religious hypocrite. I don't profess to believe in God and call myself a Christian then live my life as a sinner while turning away from doing Christian acts. I know many that do but I am not their judge. Personally, I would much rather be condemned as a doubter as to live as a religious hypocrite. It gives me more respect for myself.

When defending how God came to be, the religious answer is that he always was. Without having the faith that this is true it is a very hard concept for me to believe. I cannot imagine a spirit of some kind that, always was, setting there in the dark deciding to use an almighty power to create the universe. There is a conflict when trying to decide if the Christian God is a spirit, a man image, or both. Some religions refer to him as a spirit but man was supposed to have been created in his image. If he is just a spirit how can we accept that he has a gender and is referred to as a male.

It is just as easy, without having to rely on faith, for me to believe that if God always was then so could have been the universe and no spirit or Supreme Being had to create the universe. Some try to make us believe that the universe could not have always been as it is made of matter and matter cannot just exist. I say if this is true then you prove to me that God existed before the universe was created without using faith as the primary basis.

If the universe always was and its creation did not happen then everything else that is here today could have happened through evolution. There is also a possibility in my way of thinking that if the universe always was then there could be other valid scenarios as to how mankind began on earth besides evolution and creation, however, I will not address these other possibilities.

I base my thoughts on us not really knowing how old the universe is and knowing that evolution is a scientific fact or something is wrong in real life. Take the simple example of canines. Science tells us that all canines evolved from the wolf. It is readily apparent that there is substance to evolution or we would not have so many new breeds that have come to be in recent history. If genes can be manipulated by breeding and science there is no good sound reason not to believe the same could happen naturally over time with all species. The natural manipulation may have been due to changes in environment. Almost all domestic animals fit into this scenario.

Then look at the diversity of human beings. I know how the Bible explains the diversity of humans but it does not make as much sense to me as does evolution and environment.

We can see with our own eyes how much of the land as we know it today evolved to its present day form through erosion, volcanoes, and other natural forces. God did not make the Grand Canyon in its present state of being. You may say that it is in its present state because that is the way God wants it but to me that takes faith.

There is some scientific evidence that a caveman probably did exist. Doesn't that conflict with what is not in the Bible? If a caveman type of creature (man) did exist then how can it not be addressed in the scriptures? I believe it is probably because the people who wrote the Bible were not knowledgably enough to have known about the caveman. I am not going to say that we ascended from the primates (the possibility does exist), as I just don't know but anyone who has watched the great apes should be able to admit that there is a lot of resemblance and we do have a tail bone and we also have an appendix that may have had some use in the past such as part of the digestive system when man's diet may have consisted of more tree leaves and stems. Doctors say that the appendix has no function today and cannot fully explain why we have an appendix.

Science has yet to confirm what they refer to as the missing link but this could change in the future if the missing link is found. Somewhat like the credibility of the flood if the ark is ever found. However, considering the size the ark must have been compared to a man size object it seems that the ark would be much easier to find.

I do not have the faith and imagination to accept creation the way the bible says it happened. I think instead that early man, as does present man, searched for an answer to his being. Being uneducated and knowing nothing of science his earliest ideas must have turned man to a supreme or superior force that created what was in his world. This would not have been the Christian God of the Bible in my opinion as the earliest hints of worship were of objects or events.

As time passed and others searched for answers I believe the early stories that later became parts of the Bible started being told around the campfires and was passed from generation to generation. With each generation adding embellishment along the way until such time that man could use a language to start writing about the stories. Much the same, as what we know to be true that the Native Americans used to keep spirits and traditions alive within their culture. Some Native American tribes had no written language and passed down their culture through stories and pictures.

History has produced philosophers, thinkers, and leaders as far back as the written word and probably before. Since faith is not required it is easy for me to imagine someone like Moses who was the leader of his people and could have easily convinced his people that he talked with who became the Christian God written about in the Bible. It is then not hard for me to believe others may have enhanced these stories until they were finally accepted as the truth. As leaders they were able to lead their people to do all the different things talked about in the Bible. There is positive proof in history and modern day how others will follow someone they believe. Just look at Hitler or Jim Jones or any other religious cult.

The story of the flood could be possible, as interpreted by the time, but what caused the flood may have not been God's doing but instead it could have been caused by a tremendous tidal wave caused by a meteorite landing in the ocean. Science has a theory that this is what may have also caused the demise of the dinosaurs. An event of this type could have also caused many days of rain. Since the Ark has never been proven a fact by being found it may just be another story to justify a real flood of the time.

The Bible where I looked does not address how or why we have ravens today. There is no mention that I could find of the pair taken aboard the Ark having off spring, yet Noah first let a raven go in search of land before he let the dove go and the raven never returned. So how do we have ravens today? Anyway, it is just another inconsistency that lends itself to doubt by those like me that is not willing to accept the Christian word by using faith. Other things such as the parting of the Red Sea may also have been caused by a natural disaster or it could also just have been another story in the Bible.

In all my discussions with religious people when I ask for proof of God it always comes back to "You have to have faith in God's existence". It seems to me that if God is real that there would be proof positive so man would not have to rely on faith. If this proof existed we would not have all the conflicts and different religions that exist today.

Why would the Christian God want civilization to be so divided by religious beliefs if he is all about love and acceptance of one another? If positive proof were available Christians and Jews would not have to fear the Muslims, as is the case today. Muslims would not find it their duty to kill and destroy non-believers to their religion. This may someday cause a religious war here in the U.S. if the Muslims continue to kill Jews and Christians. It is something that should be closely watched, as Islam is the fastest growing religion in the U.S. based on what I have read.

Actually, I believe if proof was available we would probably have only one religion and everyone would probably believe the same, as proof would dispel any doubters and Atheist. Most, if not all, would agree on the proof and accept whatever it proved and the few who didn't believe could be ignored or banished. Yes, I know we are not suppose to question God but I think positive proof would do away with world differences. If you look at the root cause of almost all wars and conflicts throughout history I think you will find an overwhelming amount stemmed from religious differences.

Those who believe in the Bible and have the faith to believe what is written must defend the written word as the truth. I can understand this. However, it bothers me as to why there are so many different religions and so many different kinds of churches within the religions. If the Bible is the true word then why doesn't all religions use the Bible as the book of truth? Why doesn't all religions agree on the life of Jesus?

Jesus is another story that is hard for me to accept if he was supposed to be the trinity. If he was really God and the Son of God as part of the trinity then why was it necessary for him to have had a childhood. He could have come as a grown man and did his miracles and his preaching, as he should have had the power to do that. I think it would have made his life more believable, as how else could he have suddenly appeared as a man with no childhood. Jesus was supposed to be a carpenter but there is little reference to anything he ever did as a carpenter. When did he work as a carpenter and for how long? When he returns, as the Christians believe; is he going to return, as he was when he died, as a baby again, as an old man, or perhaps as a spirit picking out the chosen for the rapture.

I believe that there very well may have been a man named Jesus that was of that time and I really have very little reason not to believe that he was a religious person and had followers. However, I do not necessarily accept the miracles as described. I think it is possible that stories may have been told that would have made him look really great, as it was his followers that told the stories about him that are in the Bible. If I were following a person then I would want to justify why I choose to follow that person. I think that the man named Jesus was probably crucified as told in the Bible but I am not convinced that he rose from the dead.

Again, here you must have faith that this happened. I think it may be possible that because his followers believed him to be the Son of God that a plot to remove his body from the tomb was enacted to convince others that he was who they said. I think there was a great need for his followers to try and convince others that being the Son of God was the only way he could have left the tomb. I think they may have been capable of doing anything necessary to enhance the teachings of Jesus. Otherwise, the word of Jesus may have died with Jesus. It is also possible that it is just another Bible story.

You see, without the necessary ingredient of faith people like me question some of these stories. I know it is hard for Christians who do have the faith and believe all that is written in the Bible to understand my kind of thinking. I know it makes them angry when doubters like myself question the word of God. They believe so firmly and have so much faith that they cannot understand how anyone cannot believe. I know it is easy for them to accept what is written. They must accept it or they would question it just as I do.

Why has God not talked to anyone in so very long that would be valid enough to add to the Bible? History continues to be written so why is the Bible not also updated by modern day talks with God by the modern day likes of Moses, Noah, or Abraham. I don't know who that may be but I am sure there should be some in the modern world that would qualify. Is mankind supposed to just accept the thousands of years of old stories in the Bible with no updates? Seems far-fetched to me. Oh, I have heard of a lot of preachers and men and women of religion claim that God came to them and talked to them but why is it not a widely enough accepted and validated event that it becomes part of modern day religion with Bible updates?

Another thing that is hard for me to comprehend is the selective prayer that some believe to have been answered and the acceptance of so called miracles. If you have two equally religious people who are praying for the life of a loved one to be spared and one life is and the other is not, then, other than the old religious standby of not questioning God, how do you explain why one died and the other did not. When it comes to miracles there is a wide range of so called miracles that do not make sense to me. Let's say a building collapses in an earthquake. Hundreds of lives may be lost but someone is pulled from the damage still alive because part of the structure saved the person from being crushed and most religious people call it a miracle. I cannot accept this as a miracle. It is just a fact that often happens in disasters. If it was truly a miracle I would think all lives would have been saved not just one.

Why do so many that claim to be Christian not live and share as religion teaches? Let's take for instance the ultra wealthy that claim to be such good Christians. I am not talking about the person that may have a few hundred thousand dollars, I am talking about the ones with millions and hundreds of millions who do not share the wealth as a good Christian should. Sure some may give a little to charities but I believe in most cases that it is the tax deduction not the kindness that is the main motivator. You may say the Bible does not say your wealth must be shared as a Christian act. I do not know, as I do not know the Bible that well. However, I believe it would be the Christian thing to do. There is the story of Lott who was not even a rich man but shared with complete strangers to the point where he lost his home and his wife.

No human being needs hundreds of millions of dollars but there are hundreds of millions of children who need humane living conditions. A few million dollars from each of the ultra wealthy who claim to be Christians would help so many children have a better life and in return they could give back to society. The way it is now they either die as children or if they do obtain adulthood they certainly will not, in most cases, become assets to society. Instead they will continue to survive by any means necessary, as survival is the most basic need of any specie. I believe being a Christian is far more than believing in God.

I am not talking about just the third world children as we have mountains of poverty right here in the inter cities and less civilized rural areas of the USA. In terms of some individual's wealth, think how little it would really take to build and maintain, with safety, play areas and educational facilities in some of these areas of poverty. Many have none or very little and in most cases those that do exist are left to run down and become infested with the criminal element. States and local governments cannot afford to take up all the slack without raising taxes even more and they may also not really care. On the other hand the ultra wealthy could do this and the impact to their wealth would be like a couple of dollars to most of us. They know who they are and none of them in my opinion should profess to be Christians without proving how much they care with what I consider to be Christian acts of sharing. Perhaps someone from a TV talk show could understand what I mean.

The plight of the children in the world is another reason I find it hard to accept a belief in God. How can a supposedly merciful God allow so many children to suffer so much? If he is so all knowing he must know how hard the pain is to bear by innocent little children when the hunger is so intense that they bend over in pain. If he loves children so much then why does he make so many of them suffer. Oh, I already know the basic answer that a Christian would tell me, as I have heard it a thousand times. In my opinion that does not answer the why.

Another thing that really yanks my chain is all of the TV preachers. Others may disagree with me but I think the majority of them do it for the money not for their love of God. To see them rant and rave about their religious feelings trying to appear so honorable and God fearing then reading about them caught up in some scandal. It sure happens a lot. I know I am not their judge but that does not keep me from having my opinion about them.

I cannot answer, as to when I became doubtful of a Christian God, as it did not happen over night. I was raised by a Christian Mother and a Father who enforced my Mother's desire that we children attend Sunday school and often church services. At one time I enjoyed going to church and Sunday school and especially liked Vacation Bible School. My belief lasted all through my teens and I prayed a lot going through Air Force Boot Camp where I even served my flight as Chapel guide. I was still very uneducated and really had not seen much of the world at this time of my life and having been raised in a more or less Christian home I had no reason to doubt what I had been taught.

Since then I have watched a lot, read a fair amount, and seen the daily lives of many in ports such as Hong Kong in the 60s. As I observed young toddlers on the streets of Hong Kong living in filth and squallier with no obvious parental control I wondered how God could let these kind of things happen. These sightings were not in the middle of the afternoon when parents may have been trying to scratch out a living. It was at all hours of the day and night. At night you could see some children sleeping in the doorways of businesses closed for the day with no obvious parent in sight. Some of the little tykes would come up to you (as I think they learned very soon in life what the Navy uniform looked like) and tug at your pants leg begging for handouts. Most looked very sad and forlorn but it was obvious that they were dirty and hungry. Some would try to give you a smile but it was easy to see they had little to smile about. It was really heartbreaking and it was hard to understand. The gift of a few Hong Kong dollars would produce an even bigger smile. In your heart you would hope that your little gift might sustain them another day. I think times like this may have been what prompted me to begin questioning the Christian God that is supposed to be so merciful.

Later as I seen more, read more, and had more life experiences the doubt grew and I lost the ability to believe based on faith, as I now pretty much rely on proof and facts in most of my beliefs. I also base a lot of my beliefs on what I consider to be logical possibilities.

I hold no animosity toward anyone who has the strength to hold onto the faith that is required to believe in the Christian God and I know many that live a pretty good Christian life, at least on the surface. I wish that more Christians could accept non-believers as readily as non-believers are willing to let Christians believe what they want to believe but that is not the case.

Most believers are ready at the drop of a hat to condemn those who do not believe as they do. As I mentioned before one popular religion even believes they should kill anyone who does not believe in their religion. I have had jobs where if my boss knew I was not a Christian I probably would have been fired. I have most often had to remain silent in the work place, as so many professed to be Christians but they often forgot that their actions do not confirm what they claim and one sees it often in the work place. It is not easy to be a doubter, as so many find it unacceptable yet they are very hypocritical in their actions after condemning the doubter. Things like cheating on their spouse, lying about work accomplished, and drinking and swearing like sailors to name a few.

I do not try to sway others to think the way I do and I agree with several of the commandments, as I think for the most part they are good guidelines for any society to live by. Of course the Jewish faith believes the original commandments was a covenant that God made with the Jews. The versions seen in most Christian religions differ somewhat from the Jewish version. I don't think one has to be a Christian to accept a civil life style when it comes to things like murder.

In my opinion I live as a pretty decent human being for the most part and when I can afford to I give to charities even though I suspect that most of the time the administrators are walking away with much more than goes to the actual cause. I have compassion for those less fortunate than me. I don't believe I am mean or evil. Maybe a little rude at times. Doubters and non-believers are not usually evil as many would like to think. Most of us just find it hard to accept Christianity without more proof and less reliance on faith.

We are the ones who will pay the price if we are wrong. If it turns out that we are right then believing will not have jeopardized a Christian's final destiny. Believers have every right to try to convince doubters to change as long as it is not done in a harassing way. However, I don't think they have the right to condemn doubters and non-believers.

I don't know what will happen to me when I die. My belief is that it will not matter, as I don't believe in Heaven or Hell. Many will say at this point that I definitely will go to hell. They may be right but if God is real then only he can make that decision and if he is not real then it truly will not matter.

I am not overly impressed with the nature of being in heaven as told to me by some Christians anyway. It does not seem that just floating around as a spirit with no arms or legs, or cars to drive, or egg salad sandwiches and milk to eat and drink, or TV to watch would be all that exciting. Not being able to hug a family member or a friend would not appeal to me. I would miss the mountains and the woods, the rolling plains, and the wild flowers in the spring. On the other hand, if hell is just a place where your spirit is continually burning one will not have to worry about cold winters and since there is no water it should be a dry heat.

Since no one alive has ever been to either place and only have his or her beliefs to judge each by then I don't have to worry about what they think, as they do not know anymore than I do. I cannot tell you at this time if on my deathbed that I will change my mind and not take the chance but I would hope that I would be firm in my belief or non-belief whichever way you would care to say it. Chances are good that I won't have to ponder that question as many deaths come very rapidly. If I am buried and have a head stone then whoever orders my headstone can have written on the headstone, "Now He Knows For Sure ".

Chapter Seven
<u>Potpourri</u>

This chapter contains a selection of issues that I have an opinion about but I don't know enough about them to really justify any of them as a stand alone chapter or they do not need much to justify my opinion.

<u>Speaking English</u>

This issue should anger all <u>citizens</u> of the Republic. This country could have been founded by any number of nationalities who did not speak the English Language and we could have had Chinese, German, Spanish or any other of hundreds of languages as an official language but that was not the case.

We were founded by mostly English speaking people and all of our early documents were written in English. The Constitution and Bill of

Rights were written in English and they make up the most important document that has ever been written in the world. English became the official language through using it to write all of the founding documents to include the Declaration of Independence.

As immigrants came from all areas of the world they understood that they had to learn the English language to be productive citizens of the Republic. Most never hesitated. Even the slaves who had not freely come here had to learn to at least understand English. The common language is what allowed this country to grow so rapidly and for the citizens to be able to communicate so effectively. Even the Native Americans learned some English in the early periods of the country.

If the common language would not have been accepted by all then we would have ended up with pockets of people who could not understand each other's language and nothing would have ever gotten accomplished. This would automatically have kept us divided as a people. You can look at the UN to see the problem multiple languages can cause. There are nasty trends going on that may take us back there.

I have absolutely no problem with anyone that speaks other languages and admired any who can speak more than one. I think it is just fine to speak whatever language you want in the company of others that speak that language. However, I do consider it rude to carry on a conversation with someone in a language that is not understood by all present in social situations.

I have traveled all over this great country and until just a few years ago I never had a problem communicating with people no matter where I went. That is rapidly changing and it is going to drive another wedge of division in our country. Many of the immigrants coming to the U.S. now make no effort to learn English. Instead, they demand that we use their native language to communicate with them. We must not allow that to happen.

As a United Nation it is imperative that we maintain an official language and because of the long tradition of considering English our official language I believe this should be our official language and made official by whatever means is necessary. Many in our government do not think this is an issue and I can understand why, as most of congress is so far out of touch with the average citizen that they have no idea the problem it is causing.

Congress will not do anything until the citizens bring enough pressure to them. We must as a unified people demand that congress makes English the official language of this country. Everyday more and more states and local governments are facing added unnecessary expenses to accommodate non-English speaking people.

In recent years many states and local government have bowed to the pressure and started printing ballots, signs, forms, publications, and on and on in English and Spanish as well as even a third language in some areas where third language peoples are concentrated. This is expensive and they should not have this extra burden placed on them. They in turn have to raise your taxes to pay for the added expense. The federal and some state governments are printing thousands of documents in both English and Spanish. Some of these documents are several hundred pages in length. This practice at least doubles the printing cost not to even mention the double use of our natural resources used in the printing industry. People, your taxes have to pay for this.

Before this double expense gets completely out of hand we need to demand that official documents, publications, books and anything official either federal or state be printed in English only. For those who do not read or speak the English language they should have to use their own resources to have an interpreter explain the document. In many cases this could be a friend or family member who have learned the English language.

They will then understand the need to learn the official language. As long as we cater to them and bow to their every need by having bilingual printing and bilingual employees in public and government places they will not bother to learn the English language. If you cannot understand the division this causes you need to go into an area where no one speaks your language and try to communicate. You will quickly learn the division present because you cannot communicate with them. They have come to this country of their own free will and they must be forced to learn the language needed to communicate.

Why should our public servants have to learn another language in order to communicate with citizens that does not speak or understand the accepted language of the country? It can cause problems that can result in death. Imagine a police officer trying to communicate with a person that cannot understand what they are saying. If that person makes an aggressive move it could result in their death. On the other hand, consider a person injured in an accident that cannot communicate with the emergency personnel. It is not right or fair that the public servant should have to learn several languages in their own country. It is the responsibility of the citizen to learn the accepted, and what should be the official language of the Republic.

I caution you not to ignore this. We need to make sure congress corrects this monster as soon as possible.

Public Schools

I do not know when the prime was for public school in this country but they were still pretty good in the 40s and 50s when I went to school. I never attended public schools in the large cities so I don't know how they were during the above period. I think most received a fairly decent education. I think all of us who graduated or learned enough to pass the GED could at least read.

My daughters attended public schools in the 70s and 80s so I know by then that they had declined in quality. What I see today in the public schools is disgraceful. After the first few grades most of the children have very little respect for the teachers and in some public schools starting in middle and junior high the children are down right disrespectful. It gets even worse in high school. I have been a substitute teacher in two different districts, one large and one small, and both have the same problems in my opinion.

I believe the root cause of the deterioration of the public schools is the intrusion by the Federal Government. It seems that anything the feds get involved in ends up in a shambles. They <u>always hold</u> the treat of losing funds for non-compliance of the rules and regulations they pass down. The problem with most of these rules and regulations is that they are enacted based on political correct ideas. Political correctness is another tool used to divide people.

Federal rules and regulations have made it almost impossible for the administrators to have any control on discipline, curricula, food service, and many other parts of the system. The feds seem to have their dirty little hands in every aspect of public schools teaching your children. I don't know when the feds were able to get this chokehold over state control of public schools but probably when the Department of Education was created in 1979.

I could continue to try and use my thoughts and opinions about public schools but instead I need to refer you to one of the best articles I have ever read about the present situation. If you will take the time to read the referenced document it will give you so much insight to the problem.

The following is what all citizens interested in their children's education in public schools should use as a starting reference to understand how the Federal Government is ruining public schools:

Cato Handbook for Congress Department of Education

http:\\www.cato.org/pubs/handbook/hb105-11.html

You should be able to find it on the Internet by using key words Cato Handbook for Congress.

As citizens we should demand from congress that they dissolve the Department of Education and return control to the states. For those who care, remember it was the feds that took the right of prayer out of the public schools. It is within our power to force congress to act if we care enough. Under the present system I believe the public school system does much more harm, than good to our young.

Professional Entertainment

Professional entertainment includes all entertainment to include sports, music, movies, and television. They all make up most of our entertainment in this country and affect so many aspects of our daily lives. I guess why I choose to write about them is because of the way they seem to distract us from issues that should be much more important to us as responsible citizens.

Ray Reeves

I like to watch a good football game or a good golf match but I have little interest in any of the other professional sports. I like a lot of different music but I have never been to a concert, and can't stand to listen to some music. I can take or leave most movies and have no idolized movie star. Even though I watch many hours of TV, most days, other than the History Channel, and documentary type shows I find only a few shows that I really like. The others I watch waiting for the ones I do like to come on or just to have something to occupy my time. I often awake from naps due to the boring content. So you have an idea that professional entertainment does not control my life and you can probably understand why I am ready to criticize professional entertainment.

Let me make one blanket statement about professional entertainment. The players or stars are vastly over compensated for their participation in my opinion. I realize this will probably never change as fans will continue to pay out the nose for a chance to see their favorite personalities and that is what allows the players and stars to continue to get outrageous compensation. It is also why taking a family of four to a professional ball game can easily cost over $100.00. Recently, a baseball player was given a $99 million dollar contract for ten years.

I know all citizens have the right to free speech and I am a big defender of that right. However, for some reason it really gets under my skin for well-known personalities to voice their opinion about different things, as they have too large of a forum compared to the average citizen. Because so many of them are idolized by so many fans I think they have too much influential power in what they spout. This leads the fan to believe what the idol says instead of getting the facts from more reliable sources.

I wish as a general guideline that they not use their position to express their views even if I agree with what they say. I realize this is somewhat hypocritical of me to say since I am also voicing my opinions in what I write, however, I doubt that my forum will ever come close to reaching as many listeners or readers as does the famous. If they just write their opinions in a book then I think that is much fairer.

I also wonder why so many of them are so irresponsible in their actions in their daily lives. They have so much in the way of material things or the ability to obtain material things but yet they will ruin their lives by using drugs, killing spouses, beating up spouses, and other acts that disappoint their fans and in many cases finishes their careers.

You may say that happens in all walks of life and I agree but in the other walks of life not near as many will be affected such as the fans. In other walks of life they may not have near as much to lose in respect to material wealth and famous careers. However, when you consider the numbers then the famous have a larger percentage of incidents, as does the non-famous. It seems to me that they should always be on their best behavior. I think the reason they are not is that they really believe they are above being scrutinized, blamed, or in some cases above the law and therein lies the problem.

If the average person would be as aware of what is going on around them in regards to the government, laws being passed, tax increases, crime in their neighborhoods, and other things that really affect their daily lives, as they are aware of what ball games or movies are playing we would not have the interference in our lives from the governments that we have. If they would listen to a couple of hours of talk radio while commuting instead of some musical station with almost non-stop commercials. If they would watch a political debate once in a while instead of a sitcom rerun they would have a better idea of who to vote for besides a party. They might even see the need to vote instead of not voting.

If the average person would watch a documentary on something that affects them and future generations instead of spending $10.00 on a fictional movie they would have a better idea of things that may have a large affect on their children and grandchildren in the future.

I just think that the average American spends too much of their time, money and effort on the entertainment offered by the professional entertainment industry instead of becoming more aware of things that affect their lives so deeply. Professional entertainment is a diversion very beneficial to the government to keep people from seeing what they are doing behind our backs. If we are at a concert or watching a ball game instead of watching Cspan then we cannot be aware of what is going on in congress and I promise you congress needs watching.

<u>Gays, Lesbians, and Marriage</u>

I guess I will take a stab at this, as it has become a real issue lately. I don't know a whole lot about homosexuality but I have read some and watched a couple of things on TV and like many things I have my opinion. There is really no need to close our eyes to it and pretend it may go away. Homosexuality is here and unless they are all locked up or killed they are going to be here living among society. Even if one of the above was done there would still be some under cover and we sure can't do either worldwide.

Ray Reeves

My biggest question is why would someone choose to be homosexual? It does not make sense. That leads me to believe that some of the research that claims homosexuality is caused by a gene defect or a chemical imbalance could be true. They really may not have a choice. They may be pulled toward the same sex much, as is the alcoholic pulled toward the alcohol. Science has determined, and it has been accepted, that alcoholism is a disease. Why would anyone choose to live a lifestyle that approximately 75 to 80 percent of society in this country condemns. This is based on research that claims 10 to 20 percent of the population may be homosexual. This could be understated, as there may be a lot more in the closet that the research didn't catch. It also may not include bisexuals.

I have heard some well known religious personalities say that it is a chosen lifestyle and they could quit if they wanted. I imagine any of them could choose not to participate in homosexual activities just as one who chooses celibacy does not participate in sex. However, I think that if they do choose to be sexual that their feelings and desires are toward the same sex.

I have known a few people who were homosexual of both genders. Most I worked with and their lifestyle never seemed to affect their job anymore than other worker's lifestyle affects their job. All of them also seemed to be basically nice people. A couple of them in conversations admitted that they could not help how they felt about sexual partners. I knew one lesbian that had been in a partnership for several years with the same partner. I actually considered her a friend and still do even though I rarely ever see her anymore.

For the people that really hate homosexuals I would like to know how they would feel toward a son or a daughter or a grandchild that turned out to be homosexual? Would you disown them, expel them from you home, hate them or could you find it in your heart to accept them because you love them. I think most of us would finally choose the latter. So if you can accept the fact that one of yours could be homosexual then you should be able to accept someone else's son or daughter because everyone is someone's son or daughter.

I do not think they should flaunt their orientation as we see in some parades and protest. I think this just makes it harder for them to be accepted. I don't think they should draw unnecessary attention to themselves in public by kissing or hugging. It really has no value that can benefit them. Most of us do not like to see a man and a woman all over each other in public. So for sure we don't want to see two of the same sex in displays of amour'.

I am not sure how I feel about children being raised in a homosexual partnership. I do not know if current research has proven that who a child is raised by will influence their own lifestyle choice. It seems that if homosexuality is due to a gene defect or a chemical imbalance that it should not matter. It is possible that it is inherited and if it were then again it probably would not matter. What I would fear most is the parent trying to influence the child to be homosexual. I also think the children will have much more social pressure at school and in other social settings. Therefore, I am somewhat against children being part of a homosexual partnership until research has come to a more exact answer.

I am pretty sure that I do not approve of marriage between homosexual partners as marriage has its founding in religious ritual and I think the Bible implies it is a sin. This may seem odd for a doubter of God to write but I still believe marriage is more of a religious thing than a government thing. The religious aspect of marriage became a part of government and is defined as a man and a woman. However, I think they should be some way that a homosexual partnership can have legal status. You can call that a civil union or anything except marriage. I think it should include the same legal rights that marriage provides including the federal laws pertaining to marriage and taxes.

Our Right to Self Defense

Every human being has the right to self-defense. You do not have to be a United States Citizen to have a right to defend yourself against **anyone** or **anything**. However, if you are an American Citizen then in addition to your right as a human being you are also afforded the right under the Constitution. In addition to that we have what is stated in the Declaration of Independence: "We hold these truths to be self-evident, that all men are created equal, that they are endowed by their Creator with certain unalienable Rights, that among these are **Life**, **Liberty**, and the **Pursuit of Happiness"**. Our right to own and bear arms in the second amendment has received different interpretations depending on whether you are for or against the right to bear arms. It states: "A well regulated Militia, being necessary to the security of a free state, the right of the **people** to keep and bear arms, shall not be infringed".

I hold that Life and Liberty in the Declaration of Independence implies that I need no specific law or rule to protect my life. It also holds that I need no specific law to protect my liberty. Therefore, I have the unalienable right to protect life and liberty by whatever means is necessary. In this day and age the most practical way to do that is with a deadly weapon. My choice of deadly weapons happens to be firearms.

I believe the founding fathers considered the people as the militia but whether you agree or not it is clear that if they didn't mean **all the people** it would have stated militia instead of people. I say that the second amendment give all citizens the right to own and bear arms but even without the second amendment I have the natural human right to protect my life and this gives me the right to bear arms as my choice of self-defense.

The proponents of gun control uses all kinds of ideas, many unfounded, to try and convince others that guns are terrible things and that laws should be enacted that would really restrict gun ownership. What they really want is a law that bands gun ownership but most won't admit that because their tactic is to take little bites at a time so as not to alarm the citizens that are too busy watching TV to see what is happening to their rights.

I believe that some gun control is necessary and I have no objection to some controls. I think background checks are a good thing but I do not agree with a long waiting period. I don't think felons should be legally allowed to own firearms, if, the felony was committed using a firearm as they have proven to be untrustworthy.

Besides, if they want to commit another crime using a firearm they are going to care less if it is legal. Since I do not have complete trust of our government I don't like any controls that restrict the type of weapons we can own. If it ever comes down to a fight a shotgun stands little chance against a tank or rocket. I do not mind if firearms are registered providing that in the same law it forbids the government (this includes the police) from seizing those firearms without due process of law to include seizure under martial law. I am all for firearm ownership requiring training in the safety and use of the firearm and even annual certified qualification in the use of firearms providing the cost is kept very reasonable. I think these are good safety measures but I know if it is not a requirement that many people will own firearms that have no clue as to how to use them or how to use them safely and that makes them dangerous.

Once a person is trained, I think they should have the right to possess the firearm in his or her presence. By this I mean that one should be allowed without special license the right to have a firearm present in their home, in their place of work, in plain view on their person if engaged in activities in nature's yard such as hunting or fishing, and in their vehicle. I think this should apply in all 50 states and that there should be no law against transporting a registered firearm across state boundaries.

I think that concealed weapon laws are a big deterrent to crime, as it has been proven in all the states that have concealed carry laws. The crime rate against persons has dropped in all of those states. Therefore, I think if you are licensed in any state to carry a concealed weapon that you should have the same right in all the 50 states. For the few states that permit unlicensed carry laws some provision for an out of state permit should be enacted.

In today's world our police officers do not have the ability to protect us 24/7. On almost all police calls involving firearms, domestic violence where a firearm was used, robberies, car jacking, etc. the law arrives too late to stop the violence. Their main job then is to aid the victim if it is not to late and file a report as to the findings. This is of little comfort to the victim. The same scenario could play out even if the victim was armed but if I were that victim then I would at least like the chance to protect myself. There have been numerous cases where a perpetrator may have been stopped before much damage could have been done if the witnesses could have had the ability to stop the perpetrator. In this day and age with all of the terrorist threats that we may face daily I think it is even more important for the citizens to be armed and prepared to use their firearm to prevent terrorist activities.

Yes, we have accidental shootings with firearms and sometimes it involves children and this is tragic, however, I think that in most cases if the owner of the firearm would have had just basic training that the accident may have been averted. We also have traffic accidents, construction accidents, freak accidents, and many other types of accidents as they are a fact of life but I don't see legislation to try and ban cars. Statistics show that you are much more likely to be killed by a doctor than a gun.

Many people who own firearms never take the time to learn how to use them or how to safely store them. Some just buy them and put them in a drawer at home then most forget how easy it is for little ones to find them. Since most children are exposed to firearms at a very young age by watching TV they are fascinated by guns so it is no wonder that they will play with one if found.

I hope all of those that are opposed to firearms and rally behind gun control are never in a position that if they would have had a firearm handy and knew how to use it they could have prevented becoming a victim and maybe their loved ones too. It is too late to change your mind in the morgue.

Ray Reeves

Summary

I have tried to show the reader how much I have loved and appreciated the privilege of living in this great country. I served over twenty years in our military and was willing to give my life in the defense of our beliefs in freedom, both here and in other parts of the world, to try and stop oppression of people with the desire to be free. I love our Flag and the symbol of Freedom that it represents. I am truly thankful that I was born in the United States.

In some areas it may appear that I am anti-government and I will have to admit that I do not believe our founders who wrote the constitution had in mind the federal intervention we all have in our daily lives. There is no better country in the world in which to live, that however, does not mean that it could not be even better with less government intervention. The only other country that I might consider living in would be Switzerland.

I believe that our politics have divided this country and most of the politicians do not pass laws that are the best for the average citizen. I believe they put too much into gaining power for themselves and favor the people who pay for their elections. I believe that term limits are necessary to stem the corruptness we see in the congress. I believe their retirement benefits are far too generous. I would like to see term limits for senators put at two six year terms and representatives at four two year terms. If one serves in both houses a total of twelve years would be the maximum they could serve. Then neither could serve again in either capacity but they could serve in the Executive Branch. They should have to serve the maximum in either capacity in order to be eligible for full retirement benefits but not allowed to collect before the age of 62.

I think our tax codes are written to benefit the wealthy and the corporations in this country. I don't believe it is right to make the average citizen pay the largest burden of the cost of the nation while most corporations pay little or no tax. I would like to see tax reform approved by the citizens not the tax reform congress passes as they insist on favoring big business and themselves.

I am proud that things are changing for the better for minorities in this country especially the Blacks. I still think it took far too long for this to happen. I also hope more of them will realize that with education they do not have to live a life of crime. I encourage all ethnic Americans to accept each other's ethnicity and if you find it necessary to judge, I ask that you judge the individual not the race.

Ray Reeves

I think we are lucky in this country to have the freedom of religion or not to have a religion if we so desire. Even though I am not religious and doubt the Christian God it does not offend me for the words "Under God" to be a part of the "Pledge of Allegiance". It also does not bother me for our currency to state "In God We Trust". I am offended when doubters or non-believers are condemned by others who are believers or profess to believe. I think it is our right to believe as we wish.

I would like to see a law passed making American English the official language. I think it is important that we are not divided in any way, no matter how small, by multiple languages. I think it places an undue burden at all levels of government with unnecessary expense to provide documents written in several languages.

Basically, our public schools are in complete shambles and bear many unnecessary financial burdens due to federal intervention. I believe it is time for each state to take back their responsibility to provide public schooling. It is time to disband the Department of Education and tell the federal government to butt out of a state function. I do believe that private schools can do a lot better job than public schools at less cost. I think if the public schools were closed today and reopened tomorrow under private ownership that within five years we would rate near or at the top in education worldwide.

I hope that in the near future that more citizens will start paying more attention to what is happening in this country by being less absorbed by professional entertainment. I would like to see more responsibility by the movie makers and television producers to return to a cleaner format in what is unleashed on the public.

We live in a nation of freedoms and I think those freedoms include life style choices even if they are unpopular. I don't approve of many lifestyles that I see daily in this country but it is a right they have to live the way they see fit as long as it does not infringe on the individual rights of others. When we take away a right by law it whittles away at all rights. Each time a right is taken it makes taking another right a lot easier.

Gun control must be kept to a minimum in this country. The number of deaths caused by firearms annually does not justify stricter gun controls. Actually the controls are already too restrictive. What is needed is safer guns and gun safety education to stop accidental shootings. When all other means of accidental death such as automobile deaths are controlled, as are guns, then I may agree to stricter gun controls. Just as the automobile is made safer by such things as

Ray Reeves

air bags I also think guns can be made safer with such things as owner ID features and other smart gun methods now being invented to improve gun safety. Stricter laws on ownership and possession are not the right answer.

www.ingramcontent.com/pod-product-compliance
Lightning Source LLC
Chambersburg PA
CBHW051424280526
45785CB00003B/1151